Expectations in Financial Markets – A Survey Data Approach

STUDIEN ZU
INTERNATIONALEN
WIRTSCHAFTSBEZIEHUNGEN

Herausgegeben von Prof. Dr. Michael Frenkel

Band 14

PETER LANG
Frankfurt am Main · Berlin · Bern · Bruxelles · New York · Oxford · Wien

Jan-Christoph Rülke

Expectations in Financial Markets – A Survey Data Approach

PETER LANG
Internationaler Verlag der Wissenschaften

Bibliographic Information published by the Deutsche Nationalbibliothek
The Deutsche Nationalbibliothek lists this publication in the Deutsche Nationalbibliografie; detailed bibliographic data is available in the internet at <http://www.d-nb.de>.

Zugl.: Vallendar, Wiss. Hochsch. für Unternehmensführung, Diss., 2008

ISSN 1618-503X
ISBN 978-3-631-58560-3

© Peter Lang GmbH
Internationaler Verlag der Wissenschaften
Frankfurt am Main 2009

Printed in Germany 1 2 3 4 5 7

www.peterlang.de

For Annika, Louisa and Catherine

Acknowledgment

The subsequent manuscript could have hardly been accomplished without the persistent support of many colleagues and good friends. In the first place I would like to gratefully and sincerely thank Professor Michael Frenkel for his guidance, understanding, patience, and most importantly, his friendship during my PhD studies at WHU - Otto Beisheim School of Management. His mentorship was paramount in providing a well rounded experience consistent with my long-term career goals. He encouraged me not only to grow as an economist but also as an instructor and an independent thinker. I thank you very much, Michael, for everything you have done for me.

I am also much obligated to my actual and former colleagues at the Department of Economics at the WHU. In particular, these are Dirk Bleich, Regine Braun, Irene Delzer, Professor Ralf Fendel, Kerstin Frank, Dr. Ansgar Kirchheim, Dr. Isabell Koske, Eliza M. Lis, Claus Neuser, Nicole Reufels, Dr. Günter Schmidt, Professor Georg Stadtmann, Linda Stein, Dr. Christian Steiner, Dr. Christoph Swonke, Andreas Tudyka and Lilli Zimmermann. All of them have contributed significantly to this work. A special thank is directed to Professor Jürgen Weigand who agreed to act as the second assessor of my dissertation thesis.

Additionally, I profited from professional advice from many colleagues outside the WHU. Among them are Marcos Poplawski-Ribero Ph.D, Dr. Stefan Reitz and Professor Mark P. Taylor. Special thanks for their input, valuable discussions and accessibility are devoted to the members of DG Economics and DG Statistics at the European Central Bank, where I spent nine productive months in 2007 and 2008.

Without the constant support of my family over the course of the last years it would not have been possible to accomplish the dissertation. A deep thank has to be devoted to my parents Ute and Manfred for their faith in me and allowing me to be as ambitious as I wanted. It was under their watchful eye that I gained so much drive and an ability to tackle challenges head on. Finally, I would like to thank the most important persons in my life, my beloved wife Catherine and my daughters Louisa and Annika. Their constant support, unending encouragement, quiet patience and unwavering love were undeniably the bedrock upon which the past five years of my life have been built. Their tolerance of my occasional moods is a testament in itself of unyielding devotion and love. Thank you so much.

Jan-Christoph Rülke Vallendar, April 13th, 2009

Contents

List of Tables

List of Figures

List of Abbreviations

AUD	Australian dollar
AR	autoregressive
BAIBOR	Buenos Aires Interbank Offering Rate
BCRA	Banco Central de la Republica Argentina
BIS	Bank of International Settlement
BRIBOR	Bratislava Interbank Offering Rate
CEF	Consensus Economic Forecast
CEPR	Center for Economic Policy Research
CGG	Clarida, Gali and Gertler
CPI	consumer price index
ECB	European Central Bank
EEC	Eastern European Countries
e.g.	exempli gratia (for example)
EMU	European Economic and Monetary Union
ERM	European Exchange Rate Mechanism
EU	European Union
et al.	et alii (and others)
Fed	Federal Reserve Bank
Forw.	forward
FRBSF	Federal Reserve Bank of San Francisco
GARCH	generalized autoregressive conditional heteroscedasticity
GDP	gross domestic product
G7	group of seven
i.e.	id est (that is)
i.i.d.	independent identical distributed
IMF	International Monetary Fund
Inc.	incorporation
INT	Intervention
IPCA	Indice Nacional de Precosa ao Consumidor
IT	inflation targeting

LA	Latin-America
LLh	log likelihood
LRT	likelihood ratio test
Med.	Medium
min	minimum
MPR	Monetary Policy Interest Rate
NBER	National Bureau of Economic Research
NFA	net foreign assets
No.	number
NRNL	non remaining non-linearities
Obs.	observations
OECD	Organization for Economic Co-operation and Development
OLS	ordinary least squares
p.a.	per annum (per year)
ppp	purchasing power parity
PRIBOR	Prague Interbank Offering Rate
R	coefficient of determination
RBA	Reserve Bank of Australia
Rep.	Republic
STR	smooth transition regression
uip	uncovered interest rate parity
UK	United Kingdom
U.S.	United States of America
USD	United States dollar
VECM	vector error correction model
WSJ	Wall Street Journal

List of Symbols

Δ_1	first difference operator
E	expectation operator
f	forward rate
i	cross-section index / nominal interest rate
i^{real}	real interest rate
ϵ, ν	idiosyncratic error term
exp	eulerian number
$L(\bullet)$	likelihood function
ln	natural logarithm
p	price index (logarithm)
π	inflation rate
π^*	long-term inflation rate
ρ	smoothing coefficient
s	nominal exchange rate (logarithm)
t	time index
$\hat{y}$	output gap
$\bar{\bullet}$	long-run variable
$\bullet^*$	foreign variable

Chapter 1

Introduction

Knowing how expectations are formed in the financial markets is crucial to understanding how financial markets work. Although the market price itself reflects to some extent expectations in financial markets, market expectations cannot be observed directly. Additionally, the degree of uncertainty on the expected market price is not fully reflected by the current market price.[1] Hence, the extent to which expectations differ among market participants, i.e. the heterogeneity in the market, cannot directly be observed. Nonetheless, different strategies remain to investigate expectations in financial markets in more detail. One possibility is to conduct a survey among financial market participants. Survey data allow a detailed analysis of market's expectations as it provides information of expectations of individual economic agents. Alternatively, market expectations can be modeled within a market microstructural framework. Microstructural models assume that heterogeneous groups of market participants can be identified. The heterogeneity in the market is then introduced in the microstructural framework by assuming that the groups - while acting simultaneously in the market - base their expectations and investment strategies on different models (O'Hara, 2005).[2]

[1] However, literature educes other market characteristics to measure market's uncertainty. DeLong et al. (1990a), for instance, approximate uncertainty using the volatility in the stock market, while Trippi and Harriff (1993) use the trading volume of stocks to measure the degree of uncertainty.

[2] The most prominent microstructural models examine the interaction between fundamentalists and noise traders (DeLong et al. 1990b). While the former base their expectations on fundamentals and are considered to act stabilizing, noise traders form expectations on positive feedback rules causing bandwagon-effect and are regarded to act destabilizing.

This thesis investigates expectations in financial markets and focuses on the application of survey data. Survey data allow to directly examine the expectation formation process of market participants. The main advantage is that we do not investigate the market outcome ex-post (i.e. the actual future market price) but rather investigate the markets outcome ex-ante through expectations.[3]

The thesis focuses on the two major financial markets in terms of trading volume, namely the foreign exchange market and the money market.[4] Since these markets can be regarded as highly liquid and market participants have equal access to information (Jongen et al., 2008) this thesis is less subject to some of the weaknesses often associated with the analysis of financial markets. Hence, the foreign exchange and the money market can be regarded as appropriate candidates for an application to investigate the expectation formation process by the means of survey data. Additionally to the survey data approach, the thesis provides a microstructural model (chapter 4) to examine foreign exchange expectations in more detail.

The aim of this thesis is to analyze, first, how expectations are formed in financial markets in principle. We, thereby, emphasize whether expectation are formed rationally and consistently. Compared to irrational expectations, rational expectations are considered to have higher quality since they incorporate more relevant information in the pricing behavior (Ito, 1990). Second, the thesis examines to which extent a consensus among forecasters exists. In order to do so we examine whether the survey participants apply the same model to build their expectations. If they use different models the forecasters are regarded as being heterogeneous. The issue of heterogeneity in the market is contentious but also of interest when, thirdly, evaluating the outcome of economic forecasts. If we find heterogeneity in the market it is not unlikely that some survey participants provide consistently better forecasts compared to their colleagues. The issue of forecaster's accuracy is being analyzed by comparing the predicted to the actual market outcome for each forecaster. Hence, we analyze whether the forecast error significantly differs among the

[3] Compared to the ex-post analysis, the ex-ante analysis is superior since it circumvents possible shortcomings. For instance, market expectations represents an ex-ante measure of uncertainty, and hence, reflects actual uncertainty at a specific point in time. Contrary to that, measuring volatility ex-post does not take into account that the financial market was subject to uncertainty when the event did not take place.

[4] While the daily trading volume in the foreign exchange market is estimated of about USD 3.2 trillion in 2007, the money market exhibited a daily turnover of about 1.7 trillion USD in 2007 (BIS, 2007). This makes both markets the largest financial markets in the world.

survey participants. As a consequence, we identify forecasters who exhibit a higher capability to forecast financial and real economy variables compared to their colleagues. Fourth and finally, the thesis addresses the question whether expectations on the short-term interest rate differ among central banks. As the short-term interest rate is directly influenced by the central bank this analysis provides information on the predictability and credibility of central banks. If, for instance, the central bank frequently fools the financial market then the financial market consistently misjudges the monetary policy which is reflected in a persistent forecast error. As a matter of fact it is not unlikely that the central banks credibility suffers. In order to investigate the central banks credibility the thesis analyzes whether officially announced inflation targets are reflected in financial markets forecasts. If they are not, then market participants apparently do not believe in the central bank's policy.

This thesis is addressed to academics, policy makers and financial market participants a like. Academics should be interested to understand how expectations are built in financial markets and to which extent expectations are formed rationally. The results of our analysis are useful for academics trying to model financial market behavior. Furthermore, lecturers might be interested in whether financial market participants adopt models which are taught in macroeconomics. If macroeconomic models are reflected in market forecasts this might on the one hand encourage lecturers to emphasize its students how crucial these models are to understand financial markets. On the other hand this shows that these models seem to be well understood by financial market participants. Additionally, the analysis of expectations in financial markets is especially appealing for policy makers since they use financial market expectations to evaluate their policy actions.[5] Moreover, central banks influence market expectations through their policy actions.[6] Hence, each and every central bank should be interested in how the financial market believes in central banks's policy actions. Therefore, financial markets forecasts provide means by which the central bank can evaluate its performance as well as standing. Finally, the investigation of the expectation formation process provide evidence which might be interesting if not useful for financial market participants itself. Since we evaluate the performance of forecasters with respect to the actual development in the market as well as

[5]For instance, since central banks are aware that their policy actions affect real economic variables only with a certain time lag, most central banks react to expectations rather than to current changes in macroeconomic variables.

[6]Chapter 4 uses a microstructural model to show how expectations in the foreign exchange market can be influenced through central bank interventions. A change in market expectations ultimately yields a change in the actual exchange rate.

relative to other forecasters, the thesis provides insight information of how market participants can enhance the performance of their forecasts, i.e. to increase the accuracy of their predictions.

This thesis is structured as follows: The next chapter analyzes the expectation formation process in two foreign exchange markets, namely the dollar/euro and yen/dollar market. We concentrate on the rationality as well as the accuracy of financial markets forecasts. Chapter 3 focuses on the consistency of the expectation formation process. Since consistency compared to rationality does not require expectations to match a stochastic process generating actual exchange rates, it is a weaker and, therefore, necessary condition for rational expectations. Hence, rationality does require consistency, but consistency does not require rationality. One major outcome of the analysis is that financial market participants are heterogeneous and can be mainly classified into two different groups of foreign exchange market participants, namely, stabilizing and destabilizing traders. Therefore, chapter 4 takes this core result into account and develops a microstructural model in which the two groups act simultaneously. Within this framework we show that the central bank can effectively manage the exchange rate when misalignments of the exchange rate are generated by non-fundamental (destabilizing) influences. Moreover, chapter 4 provides empirical evidence that the intervention policy of the Reserve Bank of Australia (RBA) acts as a coordinating signal by encouraging stabilizing speculators to re-enter the market.

Chapters 5 and 6 focus on the expectation formation process in the money market. While chapter 5 focuses on expectations on the short-term interest rate for the G7 central banks, chapter 6 emphasizes on emerging markets. Moreover, 6 investigates whether the expectation formation process is different in inflation targeting countries compared to non-inflation targeting countries. Since there is a close theoretical link between inflation targeting and Taylor rules both chapters 5 and 6 analyze the expectation formation process by the means of Taylor-type rules which are frequently applied to examine the actual central bank behavior (Clarida et al., 1998; Taylor, 1999). Chapter 5 provides strong evidence that the financial market adopts Taylor-type rules to forecast short-term interest rates for the central banks of the G7 countries. Moreover, we show that certain characteristics which have evolved by the Taylor rule literature, such as forward-looking and interest rate smoothing behavior of central banks are also reflected in financial market forecasts. Additionally, we find that the financial market adopts the Taylor rule even prior to the Taylor rule literature. Compared to chapter 5, chapter 6 investigates the expectation formation process in ten emerging markets. We find that the expectations are formed significantly different under inflation targeting compared to non-inflation targeting regimes. Furthermore, chapter 6 shows that the introduction of a time-varying inflation targets provides useful information on the credibility of central banks in emerging markets. Besides this, we provide evidence that for the majority of countries financial market forecasts reflect the long-term inflation target of the respective central bank. Finally, chapter 7 concludes.

Chapter 2

Two currencies, one model? - Evidence from the Wall Street Journal forecast poll

2.1 Introduction

In empirical studies of exchange rate models, the joint hypothesis of the validity of the examined model and rational expectations is tested. Hence, one of the reasons why empirical studies often find little empirical support for the investigated exchange rate model could be the violation of the rational expectation assumption in the foreign exchange market. In fact, a number of studies have raised doubts about the validity of the rational expectations assumption in this market (e.g. Frankel and Froot, 1987; Frankel and Rose, 1995; Menkhoff, 1998, 2001). In addition, most empirical exchange rate studies implicitly follow the assumption of traditional exchange rate models which claim that financial agents can be viewed as homogenous. However, studies of the market microstructure suggest that there could be different groups of traders in the market. This led several researchers to develop models in which the rational expectation assumption is relaxed and different types of actors in the currency market are considered (e.g., Frankel and Froot, 1988, 1990; DeLong et al., 1990b).

In this chapter, we use data of the Wall Street Journal (WSJ) poll in order to compare the characteristics of the expectation formation process in two different currencies. The WSJ data set enables us to perform this comparison, because it contains not only expectations for the dollar/euro but also for the yen/dollar exchange rate. We therefore apply this survey to shed light on two aspects of the expectation formation process. The first aspect refers to the question whether the same expectation formation process applies to both currencies. The second aspect deals with the question whether there are differences between the two foreign exchange markets with respect to the homogeneity or heterogeneity of foreign exchange market forecasters.[1]

The remainder of this chapter is structured as follows. In the next section, we describe some details of the WSJ data set. In section 2.3, we examine the question whether expectations are formed rationally. In section 2.4, we investigate the expectation formation process. In section 2.5, we compare the more specific characteristics of the expectation formation process in the dollar/euro and the yen/dollar market. In section 2.6, we summarize our findings and conclude.

2.2 The WSJ data set

The WSJ regularly conducts a survey among financial market participants about their forecasts of several financial variables for a six-month horizon. The survey is published biannually in the beginning of January and July. When the survey was launched in 1981, the focus was on the expected development of the prime rate. Over time, the number of economic variables covered by the survey increased considerably.[2] Two changes in the survey are of particular interest for our analysis. First, since 1989, the survey includes a six-month forecast for the yen/dollar exchange rate. Second, in mid-1999, the WSJ added a six-month forecast for the dollar/euro exchange rate. While the survey was initially limited to 12 participants, it gradually increased to a maximum of 64 participants in January 1996 and has been very stable around 55 participants since 1997.

The WSJ data set has already been used in some other studies. However, these other studies focus on questions different than our analysis.

[1] The foreign exchange forecasters cannot be regarded as foreign exchange traders. However, they are frequently working as economists in commercial and investment banks, economic consultancies as well as universities.

[2] For example, since January 1985, survey participants have also been asked to forecast the GNP growth rate, and since 1991 the GDP growth rate. Inflation and unemployment rates have been incorporated into the survey since 1989. Additionally, since 2002 the WSJ has published forecasts of the Federal Funds Rate.

For example, Greer (2003) examines the accuracy of the one-year forecast of the 30 year U.S. Treasury bond. The analysis concentrates on the question of whether economists are able to predict the direction of change correctly and finds some evidence that this is indeed the case. Cho and Hersch (1998) analyze whether the characteristics of forecasters contribute to explain the forecast accuracy (i.e., the size of error) and/or the forecast bias (i.e., the sign of the error). While the authors do not find that the characteristics of the forecasters can explain forecast accuracy, some characteristics like the professional experience of the forecasters with the Federal Reserve System seem to be able to explain forecast direction error. Kolb and Stekler (1996) test whether a consensus exists among WSJ forecasters. The results suggest the existence of a high degree of heterogeneity so that central moments should not be used as consensus predictions. Eisenbeis et al. (2002) question the methodology used by the WSJ to construct an overall ranking of the polled economists. Since the WSJ ranks the forecasts on the sum of the weighted absolute percentage deviation from the actual realized value of each series, this methodology neglects the correlations among the variables being forecasted. Mitchell and Pearce (2007) examine the unbiasedness and forecast accuracy of individual forecasters with respect to their interest rate and exchange rate forecasts. They find that several forecasters produce biased forecasts and most forecasters cannot out-predict a random walk model.

Our study focuses on the expectation formation process in the foreign exchange market and uses the semi-annual forecasts of the WSJ data set. As we compare the forecasts for the dollar/euro and the yen/dollar exchange rate and as the former exchange rate has been included in the survey only since mid-1999, our analysis covers the time span between July 1999 and January 2005, i.e., twelve survey periods. During this time, altogether 84 economists participated in at least one WSJ survey. Hence, our data set is an unbalanced panel. In order to investigate the time series characteristics of the expectation formation process of the participants, we need to apply a minimum participation frequency of each forecaster. Therefore, we only include those forecasters in our analysis, who participated at least seven times during the period July 1999 - January 2005 in the WSJ poll. This applies to 50 forecasters of the WSJ data set.[3]

[3]As a sensitivity analysis, we also restricted our examination to those 26 individuals that participated in all twelve polls. All results turned out to be stable with respect to this adjustment. These results are available upon request. By contrast, the study of Ito (1990) - who also operates with individual data - covers only the time period May 1985 - June 1987. Hence, the time dimension in Ito (1990) is limited to a two-year horizon. The data set of Ito (1990) is updated by Elliott and Ito (1999) and covers the period May 1985 -

The WSJ data set has several advantages over other surveys and is, thus, less subject to some of the weaknesses often associated with survey data. First, the WSJ poll has been conducted for several years (since 1989 for the yen/dollar exchange rate and since 1999 for the dollar/euro exchange rate). Second, unlike some other surveys, forecasters participating in the WSJ poll do not only submit the direction of the expected exchange rate change, but forecast a specific exchange rate level. Third, from the WSJ data set we can observe exchange rate expectations of a large number of individual forecasters and not only the mean or median of a group of forecasters. This feature allows us to analyze both the time series as well as the cross sectional characteristics of the data set by applying panel econometric methods. Moreover, the individual forecasts are published together with the names of the forecasters. This allows everybody to evaluate the performance of the individual participants. The goodness of the forecasts can be expected to have an effect on the reputation of the forecasters. This should increase the incentives of all participants in the survey to submit their best rather than their strategic forecast (see Keane and Runkle, 1990).[4]

2.3 Tests for rationality of expectations

We begin our analysis by examining the question whether expectations are formed rationally. We follow Ito (1990), MacDonald and Marsh (1996), and Elliot and Ito (1999) in applying two criteria: unbiasedness and orthogonality. To investigate whether the forecasts[5] represent unbiased predictors of future exchange rates, we estimate the following relationship:

$$s_{t+1} - s_t = \alpha + \beta(E_{i,t}[s_{t+1}] - s_t) + \epsilon_{i,t+1} \tag{2.1}$$

May 1996.

[4]In contrast to the view of Keane and Runkle (1990), Laster et al. (1999) develop a model where forecasters are rewarded for forecast accuracy (in statistical terms) as well as by publicity in case of giving the best forecast at a single point in time. As a consequence those forecasters will differ most from consensus forecast whose wages depend most on publicity.

[5]It is every important to specify the information set the forecaster based his judgment on. This means that we have to specify the exchange rate level st which is used as the basis for $E_{i,t}[s_{t+1}]$. We use the exchange rate at the end of December and June for those forecasts published in the beginning of January and July. However, perhaps it would make sense to use an earlier date, since exchange rate forecast have to be collected and processed. Since we cannot specify, for each individual forecaster the specific date of his forecast, we also use a monthly average exchange rate of December and June respectively. Results do not change significantly to this adjustment and are available upon request.

Table 2.1: Test for unbiasedness

	Yen/Dollar Specification I Pooled OLS	Dollar/Euro Specification II Pooled OLS
α	-.0070**	.0170***
	(.0035)	(.0033)
β	-.0735	-.1325**
	(.0650)	(.0538)
R^2	.0028	.0115
No. of Obs.	523	523

Note: Regression results for the equation (2.1) $s_{t+1} - s_t = \alpha + \beta(E_{i,t}[s_{t+1}] - s_t) + \epsilon_{i,t+1}$; standard error in parentheses; *** (**) and * indicate significance on a 1 (5) and 10 percent confidence level, respectively.

Here, s_t and $E_{i,t}[s_{t+1}]$ denote the log of the exchange rate and the expected exchange rate at time t, respectively. In addition, subscript i denotes the individual forecaster and ϵ the error term. Unbiasedness prevails if $\alpha = 0$ and $\beta = 1$. In this case, exchange rate changes are not necessarily forecasted accurately, but the forecast errors do not show any systematic pattern. In a first step, we estimate equation (2.1) by using a pooled OLS model. The results - summarized in Table 2.1 - indicate that the constant, i.e., α is significantly different from zero and β is different from unity for both currencies. This implies that expectations are not an unbiased predictor of the future exchange rate. We also checked whether person specific constants can be identified by using a fixed-effects model. However, the test statistic did not indicate differences between individuals.[6]

We now turn to the test for orthogonality. It examines whether forecast errors are unrelated to information available at the time of forecasting. As a representation for the latter we use, for simplicity, the exchange rate change compared to the previous period. Hence, we estimate

$$s_{t+1} - E_{i,t}[s_{t+1}] = \alpha + \beta(s_t - s_{t-1}) + \epsilon_{i,t+1} \quad (2.2)$$

Orthogonality implies that $\alpha = 0$ and $\beta = 0$ so that neither a constant nor the exchange rate return of the past period can explain the

[6] As a sensitivity analysis, we also run the pooled OLS regressions with robust standard errors. This procedure also applies to all other pooled OLS regressions in this chapter. The robustness of the results of panel estimates are checked using Prais-Winsten panel corrected standard errors. None of the estimated coefficients changes in size or significance regarding this change in the specification.

Table 2.2: Test for orthogonality

Exchange Rate	Yen/Dollar	Dollar/Euro		
Specification	I	II	III	IV
Method	Pooled OLS	Pooled OLS	Fixed Effects	Random Effects
α	-.0180***	.0116***	.0118***	.0118**
	(0043)	(.0044)	(.0043)	(.0049)
β	-.1461***	.3207***	.2975***	.3168***
	(.0553)	(.0541)	(.0543)	(.0535)
Model Fit R^2	.0132	.0631	within = .0597 between = .1915 overall = .0631	
Various Test Statistics	–	–	F(49,472) = 1.42 Prob = 0.036	Hausman Prob > = .0359
No. of Obs.	523	523	523	523
No. of Groups	–	–	50	50

Note: Regression results for the equation (2.2) $s_{t+1} - E_{i,t}[s_{t+1}] = \alpha + \beta(s_t - s_{t-1}) + \epsilon_{i,t+1}$; standard error in parentheses; *** (**) and * indicate significance on a 1 (5) and 10 percent confidence level, respectively.

forecast error. In a first step, we estimated again a pooled OLS model and checked afterwards whether the assumption of a single constant is valid. As the results in Table 2.2 indicate, both α and β are significantly different from zero for both currencies. In a second step we run a fixed effects model and checked the assumption of a single constant. While the assumption of a single constant is valid in the case of the Yen, this hypothesis is rejected for the euro exchange rate. A Hausman specification test led to the conclusion that a random effects model is more appropriate than the fixed effects model. As a consequence Specification IV is our preferred specification for the euro exchange rate. However, this finding does not change our argumentation with respect to the orthogonality condition which is neither met in the yen nor in the euro.

Hence, concluding from estimating equations (2.1) and (2.2), the forecasts of the participants of the WSJ poll do not seem to support the hypothesis of rational expectations.[7] For this reason, we study in more detail the expectation formation process in the next section.

[7]This supports the results of Stadtmann et al. (2006). They use the same data set but concentrate on the dollar/euro market only. They provide evidence that expectations are biased and, hence, formed irrationally.

2.4 Examination of the expectation formation process

We examine the expectation formation process by comparing actual exchange rate developments with expectations about future exchange rates as expressed in the WSJ survey. Figure 2.1 illustrates for both the dollar/euro (left vertical scale) and the yen/dollar exchange rate (right vertical scale) the actual exchange rate at a particular point in time, st, and the average of the six-month forecasts for this exchange rate, $E_t(s_{t+1})$. While the solid line shows the mean of the exchange rate forecasts, the dashed line shows the actual exchange rate. The impression that Figure 2.1 conveys is that the mean of the forecasts follows the actual exchange rate, because in most cases the mean six-month forecast does not deviate substantially from the exchange rate at the time of the forecasts.

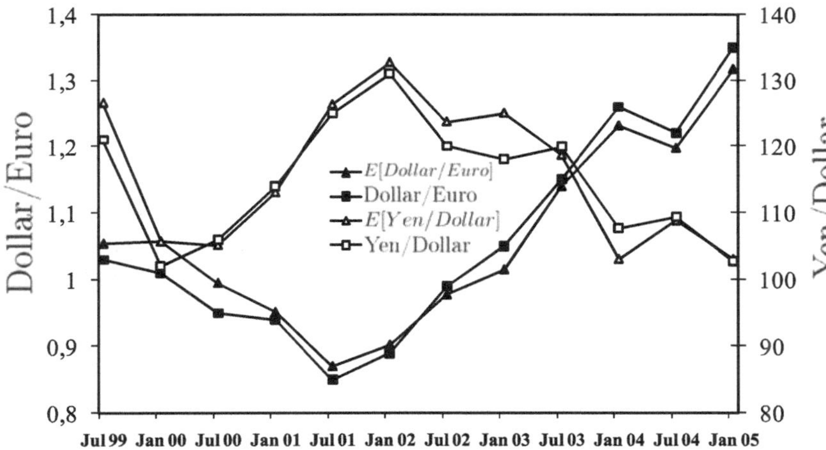

Figure 2.1: Exchange rate dynamics and exchange rate expectations

Note: Figure 2.1 shows the exchange rate at time t (s_t) as well as the mean of the 6-month exchange rate expectations of the different forecasters at time t ($\bar{E}_t[s_{t+1}]$).

In order to compare exchange rate expectations in both markets, Figure 2.2 shows the expectation of each individual i, i.e., $E_{i,t}[s_{t+1}] - s_t$ (with i = individual forecaster), for all periods included in the data set. The plot suggests two characteristics. First, the different points are grouped around

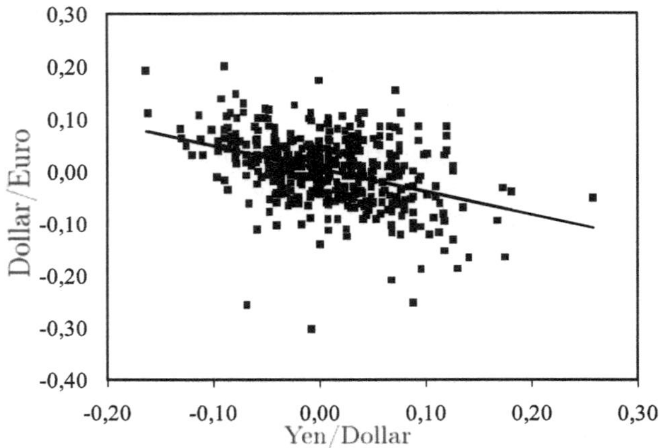

Figure 2.2: Individual exchange rate expectations in the dollar/euro and the yen/dollar market

Note: Figure 2.2 shows the expected relative exchange rate change ($E_{i,t}[s_{t+1}] - s_t$) for the Dollar/Euro exchange rate as well as for the Yen/Dollar exchange rate; the relationship between the two variables under consideration has the following characteristics:
Dollar/Euro = 0.0053** - 0.4407*** Yen/Dollar; No. of Observation = 523;
(.0024) (.0486) ; Goodness of Fit: $R^2 = 0.1647$.

the origin - the point of no expected exchange rate change. This confirms the impression from Figure 2.2 according to which expectations follow actual exchange rate developments. Second, the plot points to a negative slope which means that whenever forecasters expect, say, the yen to appreciate against the U.S. dollar (reflected in a negative value on the horizontal axis) they also expect the euro to appreciate against the U.S. dollar (reflected in a positive value on the vertical axis).

We now examine the expectation formation process more formally. We begin by investigating whether the data support the hypothesis that market participants have extrapolative expectations. Given the structure of the WSJ survey, this would be the case if the expected exchange rate change is a function of the exchange rate developments of the past period, i.e., six months. More specifically, we estimate the following expectation formation process:

$$E_{i,t}[s_{t+1}] - s_t = \alpha + \beta(s_t - s_{t-1}) + \epsilon_{i,t}. \quad (2.3)$$

If we find that β is positive this would indicate that whenever the euro,

Table 2.3: Regression results for the extrapolative expectation hypothesis

Exchange Rate	Yen/Dollar		Dollar/Euro	
Specification	I	II	III	IV
Method	Fixed Effects	Random Effects	Fixed Effects	Random Effects
α	.0091***	.0095**	.0039*	.0039
	(.0022)	(.0042)	(.0022)	(.0048)
β	-.0694**	-.0674**	-.2124***	-.2146***
	(.0282)	(.0282)	(.0281)	(.0279)
Model Fit R^2	within = .0127 between = .0319 overall =.0076		within = .1079 between = .0546 overall = .0826	
Various Test	F(49,472) = 3.81	Hausman	F(49,472) = 4.87	Hausman
Statistics	Prob = 0.00	*Prob* > = 0.4308	Prob = 0.00	*Prob* > = 0.4649
No. of obs.	523	523	523	523
No. of Groups	50	50	50	50

Note: Table 2.3 shows the regression results for the equation (2.3) $E_{i,t}[s_{t+1}]-s_t = \alpha+\beta(s_t-s_{t-1})+\epsilon_{i,t+1}$; standard error in parentheses; *** (**) and * indicate significance on a 1 (5) and 10 percent confidence level, respectively; the α-coefficient presented in table 2.3 reflects the average of all individual α-coefficients in the fixed-effects regressions.

say, depreciates, traders expect a further depreciation. In this case, expectations can be said to show bandwagon behavior. However, if β is negative this would indicate that a depreciation during the period preceding the time of the forecast leads market participants to expect an appreciation during the next period (contrarian behavior).

Assuming the same slope coefficient for all forecasters, we apply a fixed-effects model to estimate equation (2.3). The estimates - shown in Table 2.3 - imply that the slope coefficients for both currencies are significantly negative. Hence, for the exchange rate of both currencies forecasters form contrarian expectations. However, the size of the two slope coefficients differs. More specifically, if the euro (yen) depreciated by 10 percent during the last six months, forecasters expect a 2.1 (0.7) percent appreciation over the next six months. Thus, forecasters anticipate a stronger contrarian process for the euro than for the yen.

Subsequently, we examine the differences in the expectation formation process of individual forecasters. To this end, we estimate an individual slope coefficient for each forecaster. In order to present our results in a concise way, we plot the individual slope coefficients for each forecaster in Figure 2.3. Each point in this scatter diagram depicts the combination of the estimated individual slope coefficient for the euro (horizontal axis) and for the yen (vertical axis) of one forecaster. The vertical and horizontal dashed line show the estimates for the forecaster group as a whole presented in Table 2.3. Figure 2.3 reveals three main results:

- First, the slope coefficients differ considerably so that currency forecasters can be viewed as heterogeneous.[8]

- Second, while most forecasters have a negative slope coefficient and form therefore contrarian expectations, several of the forecasters have positive slope coefficients for at least one currency, some individuals even for both currencies.

- Third, there is a positive relationship between the slope parameters for the two currencies. When the slope parameter of the individual forecaster is higher than the group average for one currency, it is in most cases also higher than the group average for the other currency. This is indicated in Figure 2.3 by the numbers shown in the four areas that are formed by the two dashed lines.

A total of 20 out of 50 forecasters who have higher-than-average β values for the euro also have higher-than-average β values for the yen and 14 forecasters who have lower-than-average β values for the euro also have lower-than-average β values for the yen. However, the number of forecasters with higher values in the euro and lower values for the yen and vice versa are only 7 and 9, respectively. Another way to put this feature is the following: A regression line has a positive slope coefficient of 0.44, with being significantly different from zero on a one percent confidence interval (see the Notes of Figure 2.2). The interpretation of this result is straightforward: When forming their expectations, forecasters tend to apply a similar model to both exchange rates.

Is there a correlation between the individual slope coefficients of each forecaster and their forecast accuracy? In order to investigate this relationship we regress the individual slope coefficient on the forecast accuracy where the latter is measured by the mean squared error for each forecaster. Column I of Table 2.4 indicates that the slope coefficient for the euro is significantly different from zero, while this is not the case for the yen. In other words: Forecasters who form contrarian expectations in the dollar/euro market have - on average - a higher forecast error compared to forecasters who form bandwagon expectations.

---

[8]This confirms former research by Benassy-Quere et al. (2003). As the variables used in equation (2.3) (actual and past exchange rate) are available to all forecasters at virtually no costs, MacDonald and Marsh (1996) would define this as evidence of differences in the forecasting models.

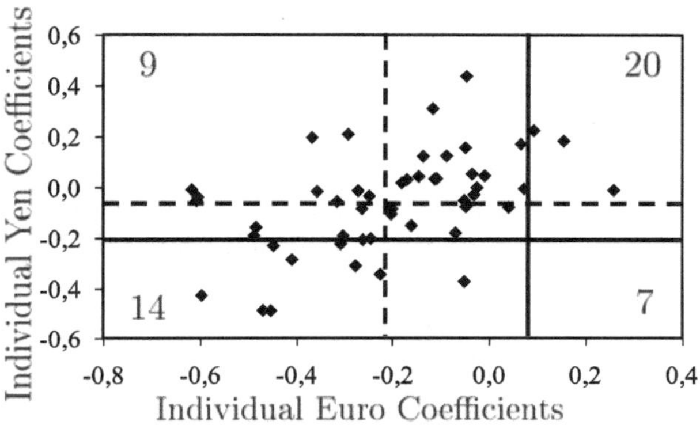

Figure 2.3: Individual slope coefficients in the expectation formation process for the euro and the yen

Note: Figure 2.3 shows the relationship between the individual slope coefficients in the Euro and the Yen. The dashed lines result from the expectation formation process and show the mean of the slope coefficient given in Table 2.3. The solid lines represent the exchange rate process, estimated in Table 2.4.

Hence we find two puzzling features:

1. There is a strong relationship between forecasting slope coefficient in the euro and forecast accuracy. However, this relationship is not present in the case of the yen.

2. Forecast accuracy is significantly higher in the case of the yen compared to the euro.

What explains these two puzzling features? To answer this question, we examine the actual exchange rate process of the dollar/euro and yen/dollar exchange rate in the next section.

2.5 Actual exchange rate dynamics versus expectation formation process

In this section, we contrast the expectation formation process against the actual exchange rate process by estimating the exchange rate change as a function of its past exchange rate changes:

$$s_{t+1} - s_t = \alpha + \beta(s_t - s_{t-1}) + \epsilon_{t+1}. \quad (2.4)$$

Table 2.4: Relationship between individual slope coefficients and forecast accuracy and actual exchange rate process

	Column I Individual slope coefficients and forecast accuracy		Column II Actual exchange rate process (semiannual)	
	Yen/Dollar	Dollar/Euro	Yen/Dollar	Dollar/Euro
α	.0093***	.0092***	.0091	.0125
	(.0005)	(.0012)	(.0247)	(.0241)
β	-.0042	-.1140**	-.2356	.0883
	(.0026)	(.0048)	(.3102)	(.2948)
R^2	.0529	.1284	.0545	.0089
Obs.	50	50	12	12

Note: Standard error in parentheses; *** (**) and * indicate significance on a 1 (5) and 10 percent confidence level, respectively; column II: Regression results for the equation (2.4) $s_{t+1} - s_t = \alpha + \beta(s_t - s_{t-1}) + \epsilon_i, t+1$.

As Column II of Table 2.4 shows, the exchange rate of the euro and the yen exhibit interesting differences. Although we find that the exchange rate is difficult to explain through past realizations of the exchange rates, the estimates point to different characteristics in the dynamics of the two exchange rates. For the exchange rate of the yen, the estimated negative value of β reflects a contrarian feature so that the yen tends to depreciate after an appreciation during a six-month period and vice versa. This is different in the case of the euro. The exchange rate return of the euro exhibits positive autocorrelation as indicated by the estimated positive value of β.

The findings on the actual exchange rate process are in contrast to the expectation formation process discussed in the previous section. While forecasters as a group assume a contrarian process for both exchange rates, only the yen exhibits such a tendency. Comparing the slope coefficients of the actual exchange rate dynamics with the expectation formation process suggests that the yen followed a stronger contrarian process than expected by the forecasters. In the case of the euro exchange rate, the actual process exhibits a positive autocorrelation, while forecasters as a group expected a negative autocorrelation for this exchange rate. Moreover, not only did they use the wrong slope coefficient, but they also used - in absolute terms - a larger coefficient for the euro than for the yen, for which the negative autocorrelation is present. Thus, they strongly misjudged the actual exchange rate process of the dollar/euro, while they were pretty close in the yen/dollar.

The results for the actual exchange rate process provide us with an explanation of why the individual slope coefficients are correlated with accuracy in the dollar/euro market, but such a correlation cannot be found for the yen: Forecasters typically applied contrarian expectations and thereby were on average more or less correct in their prediction of the actual exchange rate process of the yen (see Figure 2.3), but the same expectation formation structure led virtually all of them to underestimate the true exchange rate process of the euro.

2.6 Conclusions

In this chapter, we use the WSJ poll among economists for the period 1999 - 2005 in order to compare the expectation formation processes for the exchange rates of the euro and the yen vis-à-vis the U.S. dollar and contrast them with the actual exchange rate dynamics. In addition, we investigate whether the group of forecasters is homogeneous or rather heterogeneous. Despite the limited length of the data set, it is not subject to the typical weaknesses often associated with survey data.

Our findings suggest that each individual forecaster applies a similar expectation formation process to the exchange rate of the euro and the yen vis-à-vis the dollar. For both exchange rates, expectations are based on the assumption of contrarian behavior. However, we find that the actual developments in the exchange rate followed a different process during the period examined. The yen exhibits a process with contrarian features which were stronger than anticipated, while the euro exhibits positive autocorrelation in returns. We also find that forecasters are fairly heterogeneous confirming earlier findings in the literature. Given that the exchange rate of the two currencies did not behave in the same manner, the similarity in the expectation formation process of individual forecasters can explain why forecasters who are successful in their projections of one exchange rate path did not necessarily perform well with respect to the other currency. Additionally, we find that the forecasts are formed irrational for the exchange rates of the euro and the yen vis-à-vis the U.S. dollar. Put differently, the forecasters do not use the entire information set for their exchange rate predictions. Since rationality is a strong property for the expectation formation process, the subsequent chapter 3 investigates whether the forecasts comply with a weaker property, namely the consistency of short-term and long-term exchange rate expectations.

Chapter 3

Twisting the Dollar? - On the consistency of short-term and long-term exchange rate expectations

3.1 Introduction

In financial markets, where information is almost readily available to all market participants, it is commonly presumed that the rational expectation hypothesis holds. Especially in foreign exchange markets, which are highly developed and have large turnover, price formation is suggested to fully reflect all available information. Hence, the theoretical and empirical analysis of the foreign exchange and other financial markets often relies on the assumptions about the rationality and consistency of market participants' expectations. However, a number of studies have raised doubts about the validity of the rational expectations assumption (e. g., Bonham, 2006; Dominguez, 1986; MacDonald and Torrance, 1988; Frankel and Froot, 1987a,b; Cavaglia et al., 1993, 1994; Menkhoff 1998, 2001; Elliott and Ito, 1999; Laster et al., 1999; Stekler, 2002). Furthermore, empirical studies often find little support for the investigated exchange rate model, which can be due to the violation of the rational expectation hypothesis as suggested in the seminal paper of Meese and Rogoff (1983).

This chapter goes one step back and analyzes the consistency between short-term and long-term expectations which can coincide with irrational forecast behavior (Takagi, 1991; Ito 1993; Osterberg, 2000; MacDonald,

2000). Since consistency compared to rationality does not require expectations to match a stochastic process generating actual exchange rates, it is a weaker and, therefore, necessary condition for rational expectations. Therefore, rationality does require consistency, but consistency does not require rationality. For this reason, the investigation of consistency of exchange rate forecasts is the topic of this chapter.

We concentrate on the two largest foreign exchange markets, the dollar/euro and yen/dollar exchange market[1] and use the WSJ semiannual survey of professional forecaster. The contribution of this chapter to the literature is twofold: First, it provides evidence of forecast inconsistencies between different time horizons in both the yen/dollar and dollar/euro market. More specifically, we show that, although a relationship between short-term and long-term forecasts can be found, short-term forecasts seem to be inconsistent with long-term forecasts. Second, our results suggest that in the dollar/euro market survey participants form destabilizing expectations in the short-term, but stabilizing expectations in the long-term which represents the phenomenon of a twist.

The remainder of the chapter is structured as follows. In the next section, we characterize the WSJ data set. Section 3.3 examines the consistency properties assuming a distributed lag expectation formation with only one lag. Since this specification is not rich enough to produce a twist, we adopt a more complex lag structure in section 3.4. In section 3.5, we use a probit model to analyze whether the consistency of forecasts depends on the degree of volatility which currently prevails in the foreign exchange market before we summarize our results and conclude in section 3.6.

3.2 The WSJ data set

We use data from a survey data conducted semi-annually by the WSJ. The survey asks business experts about their six and twelve month expectations for the dollar/euro and yen/dollar exchange rate. The sample period consists of observations for the periods 1989 till 1998 and 2003 till 2007. Unfortunately, the exchange rate survey does not contain longer-term forecasts between 1999 till 2003 and has ended in July 2007. The main advantage of the

[1] While the daily turnover of the dollar/euro market is about 27 percent of the total share in the world exchange market, and hence, is the heaviest traded currency pair, the daily turnover in the yen/dollar market is about 13 percent (BIS 2007, p.10).

WSJ poll compared with other surveys is that exchange rate expectations of a substantial number of individual forecasters are reported, and not only the mean or median of a group of forecasters. This feature allows us to analyze both the time series characteristics and the cross sectional characteristics of the data set by applying panel econometric methods. Another advantage of the WSJ data set is that the poll has by now been conducted for several years. By contrast, Ito (1990), who also uses survey data, covers only a two year time period. The WSJ survey also publishes the names of the forecaster along side with their forecasts. This should increase the incentive of business experts to provide accurate forecasts and allows us to resist the reproach that inaccurate forecasts are biased due to strategic behavior rather than being irrational.

During the observation period between January 2003 and July 2007, the survey was conducted ten times and 65 professional forecasters participated in it at least once. Since we focus on the cross section characteristics as well as the time dimension, we include only forecaster who participated in all polls. This applies to 50 business experts and allows us to analyze 500 observations for both short-term and long-term forecasts, where the former refers to six month forecasts and the latter to twelve month forecasts for the respective exchange rate. The next section investigates the consistency of exchange rate forecasts using a simple lag structure in the expectations, namely extrapolative expectations with one lag.

3.3 Consistency restrictions for extrapolative expectations with one lag

In this section, we analyze the consistency properties of exchange rate forecasts by deriving conditions similar to those developed by Froot and Ito (1989). According to their definition consistency of expectations formed at the same point in time prevails if expectations about exchange rate changes during subsequent shorter time periods and expectations about the exchange rate change for the entire time period give the same result. These two forecasts will be consistent if in iterating forward, the shorter forecast $E_t(s_{t+k})$ to period $t+k+j$ gives the same number as $E_t(s_{t+k+j})$. Hence, our proposition of an internally consistent expectation formation process requires that a long-term forecast should be identical to the result of sequential substitutions of short-term forecasts, given a function of expectation formation. Hence, the consistency becomes a testable hypothesis in the form of cross equation constraints on coefficients of short-term and long-term forecast equations. We follow Frankel and Froot (1987a,b) and assume that exchange rate forecaster build their expectations by using an extrapolative model which can in it simplest form be expressed as a distributed lag function with one lag:

$$E_{t;i}[s_{t+k}] - s_t = \alpha_k + \beta_k(s_{t-1} - s_t) + \epsilon_{t;i}. \tag{3.1}$$

where s_t and $E_t[s_{t+k}]$ denote the log of the exchange rate and the log of the expected exchange rate for $t + k$ of forecaster i at time t, respectively. Subscript k denotes the forecast horizon and ϵ the error term. A negative β_k indicates that whenever the euro, say, depreciates traders expect a further depreciation.[2] In this case, expectations can be said to be destabilizing. However, if β_k is estimated as positive this indicates that a depreciation of the euro during the period preceding the time of the forecast leads market participants to expect an appreciation for the next period. In this case, expectations can be said to be stabilizing.

We follow the argument of Allen and Taylor (1990) and Taylor and Allen (1992) and consider foreign exchange traders to be heterogeneous in the sense that they consist of different types of market participants, e.g. chartists and fundamentalists. The former build their forecast on historical exchange rate changes, whereas the latter do not. Therefore, we expect that market participants apply forecast models along equation (3.1) that differ between individuals in the values of the coefficients α_k and β_k. For instance, in the case of a fundamentalist we expect that $\alpha_k = 0$ and $\beta_k = 0$. Likewise the expectation formation process of a chartists should reveal a value of β_k to be significantly different from zero.

Applying equation (3.1) to the six and twelve month horizon, which we could model as one and two periods, we obtain

$$E_{t;i}[s_{t+1}] - s_t = \alpha_1 + \beta_1(s_{t-1} - s_t) + \epsilon_t, \tag{3.2}$$

and

$$E_{t;i}[s_{t+2}] - s_t = \alpha_2 + \beta_2(s_{t-1} - s_t) + u_t. \tag{3.3}$$

By iterating the short-term expectations, the expectation of a longer time horizon can be obtained. As Appendix A shows, consistent long-term forecasts must comply with the following restrictions:

[2] We define the exchange rate change in the formulation as $s_{t-1} - s_t$ in order to derive the consistency restrictions in a mathematically convenient way.

$$(R1) \qquad \alpha_2 = 2\alpha_1 - \beta_1\alpha_1$$

$$(R2) \qquad \beta_2 = \beta_1(1 - \beta_1).$$

The interpretation of restriction $(R2)$ is quite simple. If a forecaster exhibits a positive β_1 in the short-term, say $\beta_1 = 0.9$, the long-term β_2 must be equal to 0.09 in order to be consistent with the short-term forecast. Assuming a 10 percent appreciation of the exchange rate the forecaster expects the exchange rate to depreciate by 9 percent for the next period, i.e. six months, while he expects a further 8.1 percent appreciation for the subsequent sixth months period. Overall, he predicts the exchange rate to depreciate by 0.9 percent within the next year, which is why β_2 has to be equal to 0.09.

Additionally, restriction $(R2)$ shows an interesting feature: Since the short-term β-coefficient of all professional forecasters are estimated between -1 and 1, restriction $(R2)$ states that short-term and long-term β-coefficients have to reveal the same sign in order to hold for consistent expectations. Put differently, a forecaster who forms stabilizing expectations in the short-term has to reveal stabilizing long-term expectations in order to meet the consistency restriction $(R2)$. For the econometric analysis it is also important that restrictions $(R1)$ and $(R2)$ are testable hypotheses of consistency when using the six and the twelve months forecast of our data set as extrapolative expectations with one lag.

We now apply the consistency considerations to the data set. We first estimate equations (3.2) and (3.3) for both the dollar/euro and yen/dollar exchange rate. Table 3.1 shows the estimation results. They indicate that the short-term β is significantly lower than the long-term β in both markets. This implies that long-term forecasts are more stabilizing than short-term forecasts.

In the case of yen/dollar forecasts between 2003 and 2007, the long-term β_2 (0.23) is twice the short-term β_1 (0.11). This means that a 10 percent depreciation of the yen against the dollar during a six month period leads to an expected appreciation of the yen of 1.1 percent for the next six months, while the yen is expected to appreciate during the next year of about 2.3 percent. For the time period between 1989 and 1998, we also find that β_2 (0.31) is twice as large as β_1 (0.16). This means that the survey participants form stabilizing expectations for both time horizons.

Table 3.1: Expectation formation processes of dollar/euro and yen/dollar forecasts with one lag

Exchange Rate	Yen/Dollar		Dollar/Euro		Yen/Dollar	
Period	1989–1998		2003–2007		2003–2007	
	Short-Term	Long-Term	Short-Term	Long-Term	Short-Term	Long-Term
α	.0082***	.0141***	-.0060**	-.0094***	-.0138***	-.0234***
	(.0019)	(.0028)	(.0023)	(.0031)	(.0021)	(.0032)
β	.1623***	.3087***	-.0057	.0791*	.1171***	.2321***
	(.0201)	(.0286)	(.0329)	(.0423)	(.0373)	(.0561)
Various Test Statistics	F(1,721) = 65.12 Prob > F = .00	F(1,721) = 116.21 Prob > F = .00	F(1,449) = 0.03 Prob > F = .86	F(1,449) = 3.62 Prob > F = .06	F(1,449) = 9.94 Prob > F =.00	F(1,449) = 18.64 Prob > F = .00
Wooldrigde test for autocorrelation	F(1,37) = 3.26 Prob > F = .08	F(1,37) = 2.29 Prob > F = .25	F(1,49) = .00 Prob > F = .99	F(1,49) = .67 Prob > F = .42	F(1,49) = 3.25 Prob > F = .08	F(1,49) = .40 Prob > F = .97
No. of Obs.	760	760	500	500	500	500
No. of Groups	38	38	50	50	50	50

Notes: Table 3.1 shows the estimation results of equations (3.2) and (3.3), respectively;*** (**) and * indicate significance at the 1 (5) and 10 percent level, respectively; standard errors are in parentheses; as suggested by the Hausman test we applied the fixed effects estimator; the null-hypothesis (H_0: no first order correlation in the panel data) of the Wooldrigde (2002) test cannot be rejected on a five percent level.

By contrast, the findings for the dollar/euro market is ambiguous. As Table 3.1 shows, the forecasters use destabilizing expectations in this market in the short-term and stabilizing expectations in the long-term, i.e. they expect a 'twist' for the dollar/euro exchange rate. Since this is not in line with the definition of consistent expectations used in this chapter we reject the hypothesis of consistent expectations in the dollar/euro market. The theoretical framework of a twist is the Dornbusch (1976) overshooting model, where destabilizing expectations are formed in the short-term and the long-term equilibrium is derived through stabilizing expectations.

The twisting behavior becomes more apparent in the framework of a dynamic panel estimator. We use the Arellano-Bond estimator (Arellano and Bond, 1993) to estimate the dynamic expectation formation processes with one lag:

$$E_{t;i}[s_{t+1}] - s_t = \alpha_1 + \beta_1 \Delta_1 (s_{t-1} - s_t) + \gamma_1 L_{E_{t;i}[s_{t+1}]-s_t} + \epsilon_t, \tag{3.4}$$

where $L_{E_{t;i}[s_{t+1}]-s_t}$ is the lagged dependent variable, Δ_1 is the first difference operator and ϵ_t is the i.i.d. error term. Table 3.2 shows the estimation results of equation (3.4) by the means of the Arellano-Bond estimator. While the short-term β-coefficient in the dollar/euro market is negative indicating destabilizing expectations the long-term β-coefficient is positive which points to stabilizing expectations. For the yen/dollar market the β-coefficients are positive indicating stabilizing expectations. We take this as additional evidence that expectations in the dollar/euro market are not consistently built. Additionally, Table 3.2 shows that the long-term β-coefficients are higher compared to the short-term β-coefficients. Hence, the expectation formation process reveals the stabilizing feature to a higher extent in the long-term specific. However, since the consistency restrictions derived above are obtained on the basis of extrapolative expectations with one lag we now depart from the dynamic panel specification and turn to the results obtained in Table 3.1. With the results obtained from the panel estimation in Table 3.1 we now test whether expectations in the foreign exchange market can be regarded as consistent expectations as defined in this chapter.

We now test consistency by directly estimating restrictions ($R1$) and ($R2$). The results support our previous findings. As Table 3.3 indicates, restriction ($R2$) can be rejected at least at the one percent level for both the dollar/euro and the yen/dollar exchange rate market while restriction ($R1$) can be rejected at the five percent level only in case of the yen/dollar exchange rate. Additionally, both restrictions together ($R1$ and $R2$) can be rejected at the five percent level for both currencies.

Table 3.2: Dynamic panel estimation of the dollar/euro and yen/dollar expectation formation processes

	Arellano-Bond Estimator (Two Step-Procedure)					
Exchange Rate Period	Yen/Dollar 1989 - 1998		Dollar/Euro 2003–2007		Yen/Dollar 2003–2007	
	Short-Term	Long-Term	Short-Term	Long-Term	Short-Term	Long-Term
α	0015***	0005***	.0025***	.0007	-.0015***	-.0027***
	(.0001)	(.0002)	(.0005)	(.0005)	(.0002)	(.0005)
β	.1636***	.2951***	-.0207**	.0649***	.0433***	.0277
	(.0088)	(.0117)	(.0101)	(.0198)	(.0068)	(.0224)
γ	.3565***	.5390***	.0001	.2605**	.0936***	.2768***
	(.0338)	(.0284)	(.0220)	(.0210)	(.0126)	(.0213)
No. of Obs.	684	684	400	400	400	400
No. of Groups	38	38	50	50	50	50

Notes: Table 3.2 shows the estimation results of equation (3.4) $E_{t;i}[s_{t+1}] - s_t = \alpha_1 + \gamma_1 L_{E_{t;i}[s_{t+1}]-s_t} + \beta_1 \Delta_1 (s_{t-1} - s_t) + \epsilon_t$; *** (**) and * indicate significance at the 1 (5) and 10 percent level, respectively; standard errors are in parentheses; as suggested by the Hausman test we applied the fixed effects estimator.

Table 3.3: Test of consistency restrictions ($R1$), and ($R2$)

Exchange Rate Period	Yen/Dollar 1989–1998	Dollar/Euro 2003–2007	Yen/Dollar 2003–2007
($R1$)	0.73 (.3926)	0.54 (.4633)	4.87** (.0278)
($R2$)	35.27*** (.0076)	6.81*** (.0091)	10.17*** (.0015)
($R1$ and $R2$)	18.53*** (.0000)	6.81** (.0332)	6.65*** (.0014)

Notes: Table 3.3 shows the F-values as derived from the F-test; the null hypothesis states that the consistency restriction holds; *** (**) and * indicate significance at the 1 (5) and 10 percent level, respectively; significance levels are in parentheses.

So far, we restricted β_2 to be common for all professional forecasters. We now refine our analysis by examining the relationship between short-term and long-term β-coefficients of individual forecasters. As argued before, short-term β-coefficients are expected to be related to the long-term β-coefficients via restriction ($R2$). Therefore, we first estimate the short-term and long-term β-coefficient by applying equations (3.2) and (3.3) and obtain person-specific short-term and long-term β-coefficients for each forecaster. We now regress the person-specific short-term β-coefficients on long-term β-coefficients to analyze the non-linear relationship in the following specification:

$$\beta_{i,2} = \alpha + \psi_1 \beta_{i,1} + \psi_2 \beta_{i,1}^2 + \omega_i. \tag{3.5}$$

Here, i represents the respective forecaster and ω denotes the error term. We expect that the non-linear regression line exhibit a constant term of $\alpha = 0$. Additionally, consistency would imply a slope parameter of $\psi_1 = 1$ and the kurtosis parameter of $\psi_2 = -1$. Table 3.4 depicts the estimation results for equation (3.5). We reject the null hypothesis that short-term and long-term expectations are consistent to restriction $(R2)$ at a one percent level. This confirms the results in Table 3.3 presented so far.

These findings are strongly supported by Figures 3.1, 3.2, and 3.3 which illustrate the relationship between the person-specific short-term and long-term β-coefficients for the investigated data set. They are shown as squares in the scatter diagram. Additionally, the solid line represents the estimation results obtained from equation (3.5) whereas the dotted line represents the consistency restriction restriction $(R2)$. Four results can be obtained: First, there seems to be a strong positive relationship between the person-specific short-term and the long-term β for both exchange rates as indicated by the significant ψ_1 coefficients in Table 3.4. Hence, a forecaster who puts a substantial weight on past exchange rate returns in order to extrapolate the short-term exchange rate probably also does so in the long-term. Second, although the regression line and the consistency restriction exhibit the same sign of slope and kurtosis between 2003 and 2007, the forecast behavior in both markets is significantly different from what consistency restriction $(R2)$ suggests. Third, the picture is slightly different for the yen/dollar exchange rate between 1989 and 1998. While the majority of forecasters exhibit stabilizing β_1 and β_2-coefficients, the relationship seems to be inconsistent due to the non-linear influence between β_1 and β_2. As Table 3.4 shows the regression line obtained from equation (3.5) exhibits a concave relationship, whereas the consistency restriction $(R2)$ requires a convex relationship between β_1 and β_2. Fourth, combinations of β_1 and β_2-coefficients in the upper left (lower right) quadrant of Figures 3.1 and 3.2 reflect forecaster with negative (positive) short-term β-coefficients which coincide with positive (negative) long-term β-coefficients. These forecasters exhibit what we refer to as a twist or a twisting behavior. Comparing this feature between the two exchange rates examined in our study, we find twelve forecasters with such a behavior for the dollar/euro exchange rate, while we find five and eleven business experts revealing such a behavior for the yen/dollar exchange rate between 1989 and 1998 and between 2003 and 2007, respectively. Hence, the tendency of a twisting behavior is present in both markets.

In sum, nearly a quarter of the forecaster exhibits a twisting behavior in the market for the period between 2003 and 2007. As argued above, this is internally inconsistent with extrapolative expectations with only one lag. In order to allow the twist to be internally consistent with short-term destabilizing and long-term stabilizing expectations, we need to examine a more complex lag structure in the expectation formation process. This is done in the next section.

Table 3.4: Relationship between short-term and long-term β-coefficients

Exchange Rate Period	Yen/Dollar 1989–1998	Dollar/Euro 2003–2007	Yen/Dollar 2003–2007
α	.1747***	.0945***	.1107***
	(.0292)	(.0362)	(.0337)
ψ_1	.5806**	.8532***	1.284***
	(.2537)	(.1451)	(.1678)
ψ_2	.7359	-.1745	-.4717
	(.5488)	(.2869)	(.4144)
Model Fit	$R^2 = .6030$	$R^2 = .4632$	$R^2 = .6523$
$H_0 : \alpha = 0, \psi_1 = 1$	F(3,47) = 37.32	F(3,47) = 9.90	F(3,47) = 18.41
and $\psi_2 = -1$	Prob > F = .00	Prob > F = .00	Prob > F = .00
No. of Obs.	38	50	50

Notes: Table 3.4 shows the estimation results of equation (3.5) $\beta_{i,2} = \alpha + \psi_1 \beta_{i,1} + \psi_2 \beta_{i,1}^2 + \omega_i$ for $i =$ 1,..., 50 (38); *** indicates significance at the 1 percent level; standard errors are in parentheses.

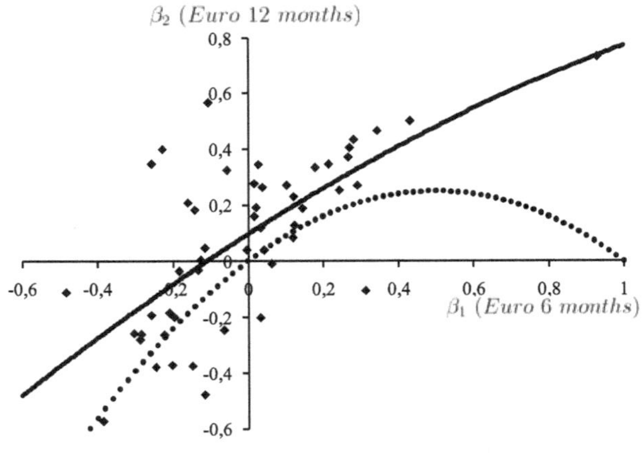

Figure 3.1: Individual β-coefficients for short-term and long-term forecasts in the dollar/euro Market (2003 - 2007)

Note: Figure 3.1 shows a) the relationship between the individual β_1- and β_2-coefficients in the dollar/euro market obtained from equations (3.2) and (3.3) as a scatter diagram b) the solid line reflecting the regression function of the non-linear relationship between β_1 and β_2 which is obtained from equation (3.5) and, c) the dotted line which represents the results obtained from the consistency restriction (*R*.2) $\beta_2 = \beta_1(1\text{-}\beta_1)$.

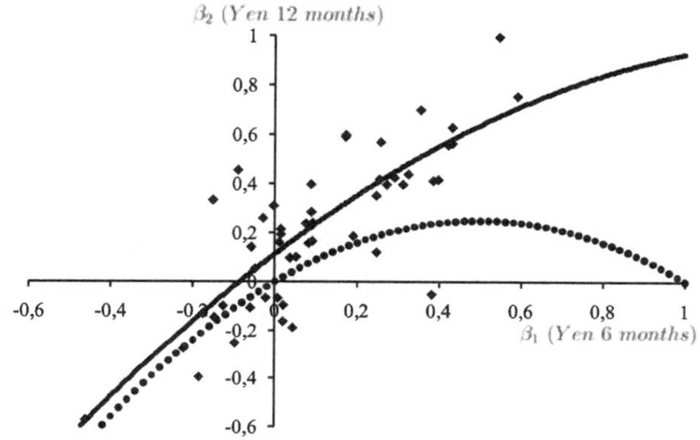

Figure 3.2: Individual β-coefficients for short-term and long-term forecasts in the yen/dollar market (2003 - 2007)

Note: Figure 3.2 shows a) the relationship between the individual β_1- and β_2-coefficients in the yen/dollar market obtained from equations (3.2) and (3.3) as a scatter diagram b) the solid line reflecting the regression function of the non-linear relationship between β_1 and β_2 which is obtained from equation (3.5) and, c) the dotted line which represents the results obtained from the consistency restriction ($R.2$) $\beta_2 = \beta_1(1\text{-}\beta_1)$.

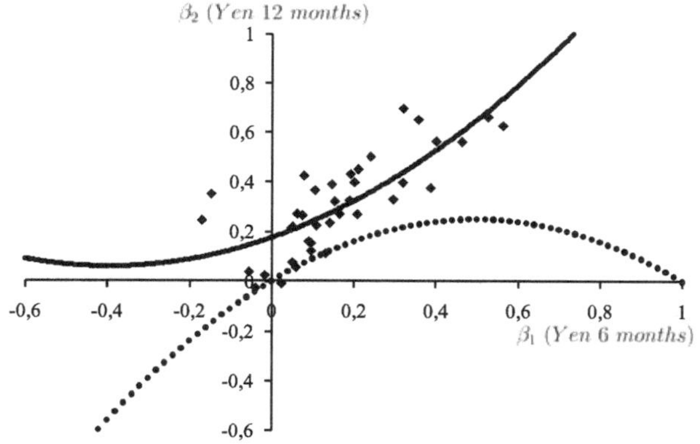

Figure 3.3: Individual β-coefficients for short-term and long-term forecasts in the yen/dollar market (1989 - 1999)

Note: Figure 3.3 shows a) the relationship between the individual β_1- and β_2-coefficients in the yen/dollar market obtained from equations (3.2) and (3.3) as a scatter diagram b) the solid line reflecting the regression function of the non-linear relationship between β_1 and β_2 which is obtained from equation (3.5) and, c) the dotted line which represents the results obtained from the consistency restriction ($R.2$) $\beta_2 = \beta_1(1\text{-}\beta_1)$.

3.4 Consistency restrictions for extrapolative expectations with two lags

In this section, we apply a distributed lag expectation formulation with two lags, which is rich enough to allow for a twist even if the expectation formation process is consistent. This means not only the change in the exchange rate between $t-1$ and t but also $t-2$ and $t-1$ affect exchange rate expectations. Hence, we consider the following short-term and long-term expectation formation process:

$$E_t[s_{t+1}] - s_t = \alpha_1 + \beta_1 s_t + \gamma_1 s_{t-1} + \delta_1 s_{t-2} + \phi_t. \tag{3.6}$$

$$E_t[s_{t+2}] - s_t = \alpha_2 + \beta_2 s_t + \gamma_2 s_{t-1} + \delta_2 s_{t-2} + \chi_t. \tag{3.7}$$

As Appendix B shows, consistent long-term forecasts must comply with the following restrictions:

$$\alpha_2 = 2\alpha_1 + \alpha_1\beta_1 \tag{R3}$$

$$\beta_2 = 2\beta_1 + \beta_1^2 + \gamma_1 \tag{R4}$$

$$\gamma_2 = \beta_1\gamma_1 + \gamma_1 + \delta_1 \tag{R5}$$

$$\delta_2 = \delta_1 + \beta_1\delta_1 \tag{R6}$$

Restriction ($R5$) shows that applying a distributed lag formulation with two lags allows that short-term expectations to be consistent with stabilizing long-term expectations even in case of a negative short-term β-coefficient. Even if forecaster reveal destabilizing short-term expectations that coincide with stabilizing long-term expectations the consistency restriction ($R5$) may hold. In order to analyze the expectation formation process in this framework, Table 3.5 presents the results of equations (3.6) and (3.7). It can be seen that, the long-term β-coefficients are smaller compared to the short-term, while destabilizing expectations cannot be found for the short-term horizon.

Table 3.5: The consistency of dollar/euro and yen/dollar forecasts with two lags

Exchange Rate Period	Yen/Dollar 1989–1999		Dollar/Euro 2003–2007		Yen/Dollar 2003–2007	
	Short-Term	Long-Term	Short-Term	Long-Term	Short-Term	Long-Term
α_k	.5197***	.6737***	-.0121*	.0025	-.8398***	-1.0596***
	(.0645)	(.0900)	(.0071)	(.0090)	(.2106)	(.32937)
β_k	-.2261***	-.4037***	.0263	-.1381**	-.0908**	-.2297***
	(.0198)	(.0276)	(.0431)	(.0545)	(.0413)	(.0577)
γ_k	.0290	.0882***	-.0694	-.0612	.0223	-.0089
	(.0237)	(.0331)	(.0452)	(.0570)	(.0483)	(.0673)
δ_k	.0901***	.1773***	.0840***	.1625***	.2422***	.4559***
	(.0201)	(.0281)	(.0332)	(.0418)	(.0346)	(.0482)
Various Test Statistics	F(3,719) = 60.54 Prob > F = .00	F(3,719) = 87.07 Prob > F = .00	F(3,447) = 3.50 Prob > F = .02	F(3,447) = 6.36 Prob > F = .00	F(3,447) = 22.08 Prob > F = .00	F(3,447) = 38.24 Prob > F = .00
No. of Obs.	760	760	500	500	500	500
No. of Groups	38	38	50	50	50	50

Notes: Table 3.5 shows the estimation results of equation (3.6) and (3.7) $E_t[s_{t+k}] - s_t = \alpha_k + \beta_k s_t + \gamma_k s_{t-1} + \delta_k s_{t-2} + \epsilon_{t+k}$ for k= 1 and 2; *** and ** indicate significance at the 1 and 5 percent level, respectively; standard errors are in parentheses; As suggested by the Hausman test we applied the fixed effects estimator; standard errors are in parentheses.

As Table 3.6 indicates, all consistency restrictions together can be soundly rejected for the yen/dollar market indicating that short-term expectations are inconsistent with long-term expectation even if one allows for two lags in the distributed lag function. Interestingly, the results for the dollar/euro market are not as convincing as for the yen/dollar market since all consistency restrictions together in the dollar/euro market can only be rejected at the five percent level. In order to investigate why expectations on the dollar/euro exchange rate are different compared to the yen/dollar exchange rate the next section analysis the impact of the exchange rate volatility on the expectation formation process.

Table 3.6: Test of consistency restrictions ($R3$), ($R4$), ($R5$), and ($R6$)

Exchange Rate Period	Yen/Dollar 1989–1998	Dollar/Euro 2003–2007	Yen/Dollar 2003–2007
($R3$)	9.90** (.0017)	6.77*** (.0096)	4.44** (.0355)
($R4$)	1.05 (.3062)	3.09* (.0795)	1.58 (.2099)
($R5$)	0.39 (.5311)	1.49 (.2234)	15.76*** (.0001)
($R6$)	21.82*** (.0000)	5.48** (.0196)	40.73*** (.0000)
($R3$ to $R6$)	8.30*** (.0000)	3.05** (.0168)	14.39*** (.0000)

Notes: Table 3.6 shows the F-values as derived from the F-test; the null hypothesis states that the consistency restriction holds; *** (**) and * indicate significance at the 1 (5) and 10 percent level, respectively; significance levels are in parentheses.

3.5 Twist and exchange rate volatility

In this section, we compare the expected exchange rate and the actual exchange rate in order to examine whether the twist in the dollar/euro market is either induced by the expectation formation process or due to the specific development of the dollar/euro exchange rate. Furthermore, we analyze why forecasters do not exhibit a twist in the yen/dollar market. As a starting point, Figure 3.4 shows the actual forecast process of the dollar/euro exchange rate between January 2003 and the last forecasted point, i.e. July 2008. In the first half of this period, the euro experienced a sharp appreciation, while in the second half of the period the euro fluctuated around \$1.25 per €. Additionally, Figure 3.4 shows, as $\overline{E_t}[s_{t+k}]$ the mean of the six and twelve months ahead forecast, respectively, over all participants. As can be seen, the forecasts are close to the actual exchange rate of the time the forecasts are made. For instance, in January 2003, when the actual exchange rate was about \$1.05 per €, the six month forecast was at \$1.031 per € and the expected exchange rate for January 2004 reached \$1.034 per €. Additionally, it is obvious that in some periods, during which the euro substantially appreciated (for instance in July 2003, July 2006, and July 2007), survey participants expected the euro to further appreciate for the six months horizon, while they expected the euro to depreciate for the twelve month horizon. In other periods, during which the euro depreciated substantially against the dollar (for instance in July 2005) the survey participants forecasted a further euro depreciation for the next six months, but they expected a subsequent euro appreciation for July 2006. Hence, the forecasters had short-term expectations that can be classified as bandwagon effects and long-term expectations that can be classified as stabilizing. This behavior is at the center of the 'twist' phenomenon studied in this chapter. As this behavior is limited to periods of sharp exchange rate movements (e.g. July 2003 and 2005), we can conclude that this is not generally the case.

Figure 3.5 shows the actual yen/dollar exchange rate as well as the mean of the six and the twelve months forecast for the yen/dollar exchange rate between 2003 and 2008. In line with the findings for the dollar/euro exchange rates, the diagram shows that in some periods actual and expected exchange rates are again close to each other. Contrary to the findings before, in most periods we cannot establish a twist in the yen/dollar expectations. However, there are only two periods in which short-term expectation are not consistent with long-term forecasts, namely July 2003 and January 2004. Specifically, in January 2004, the survey participants exhibit a twisting behavior when the yen substantially appreciated and the forecasters expected a further six months appreciation, whereas their expectations for the twelve months tended towards a yen depreciation. This supports our findings that the twist probably occurs, when the exchange rate fluctuates substantially.[3] The same results can be inferred from Figure 3.6 that depicts the yen/dollar exchange rate as well as the mean of the six and twelve months forecast for the time period between 1988 and 1999. Again, a twisting behavior can only be established in five out of 20 periods, i.e. January 1990, 1991, 1992 and July 1992, and 1996.

[3] In a theoretical framework Honohan (1984) analyzes the link between exchange rate expectations and actual exchange rate volatility. He finds that in a framework of a Dornbusch-Niehans overshooting model exchange rate expectations are more likely to be destabilizing when excess exchange rate volatility prevails. More precisely, exchange rate volatility tends to increase market uncertainty about future economic conditions and leads to a higher degree of overshooting compared to the standard Dornbusch model.

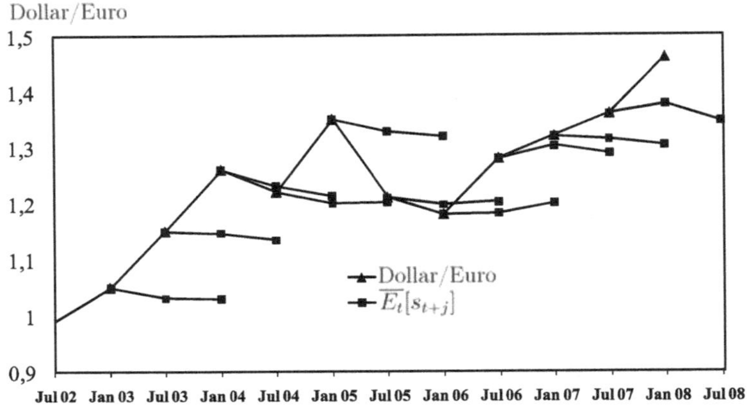

Figure 3.4: Actual and expected dollar/euro exchange rate for different horizons (2003 - 2007)

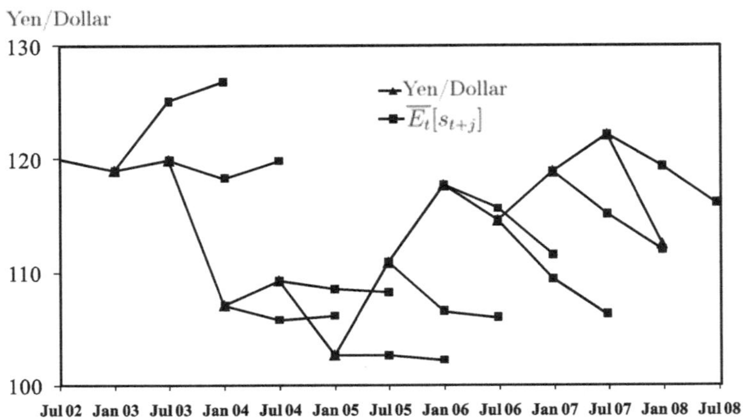

Figure 3.5: Actual and expected yen/dollar exchange rate for different horizons (2003 - 2007)

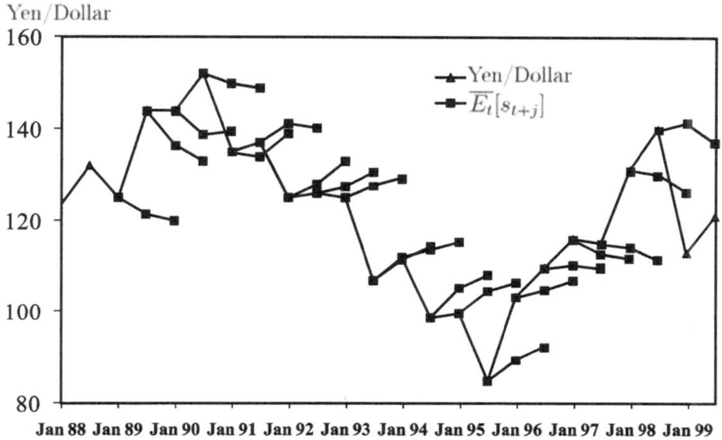

Figure 3.6: Actual and expected yen/dollar exchange rate for different horizons (1989 - 1999)

In sum, short-term and long-term forecasts of exchange rates exhibit a relationship confirming consistency of the expectation formation process. By contrast, during periods of sharp exchange rate movements the forecasters exhibit destabilizing expectations in the short-term while stabilizing in the long-term. This twisting behavior prevailed in periods after substantial exchange rate changes and occurred mostly in the dollar/euro market. This leads to inconsistent forecasts as analyzed above by applying consistency restrictions. One reason why this might the case is suggested by the noise trading literature. Since activities of noise traders who form short-term bandwagon expectations are regarded as causing excess volatility both short-term extrapolative expectations and a high degree of volatility seem to be related. Moosa and Shamsuddin (2004) use monthly data for the actual yen/dollar exchange rate and conclude that the extrapolative expectation mechanism is dominant. Moreover, they demonstrate that exchange rate volatility is linked to the heterogeneity of traders confirming our results derived above.

We now analyze whether there is empirical evidence for the hypothesis that the appearance of a twist is more likely to occur in periods after substantial exchange rate movements, i.e. in periods after high exchange rate volatility. First, we define a twist-dummy d which is set equal to one in periods in which the mean of the forecasters expect a twist whereas d is set equal to zero otherwise. For the dollar/euro exchange rate business experts expect a twist ($d = 1$) in five out of ten periods. For the yen/dollar exchange rate between 1989 and 1998 (2003-2007) this is the case in five (two) out of 20 (ten) periods. In order to test whether the exchange rate volatility - measured as $\sigma^2_{(s_t)}$ - is significantly higher in periods of a twist, we now use a (panel) probit analysis by regressing the twist-dummy d on the degree of exchange rate volatility in the following specification:

$$P(d_{t,i} = 1 \mid \lambda_{t,i}) = \kappa_i + \lambda_{t,i}\sigma^2_{(s_t)} + \nu_{t,i}. \tag{3.8}$$

where κ is the constant term, λ_t is the impact of the exchange rate volatility on the probability of an appearance of a twist in the expectation formation process of forecaster i at time t and ν_t is the error term. Table 3.7 shows the results obtained from equation (3.8) in six different specifications. Specification I to III represent the results obtained from a probit analysis on the mean of the forecasters' expectations for each sample period. As Table 3.7 indicates excess exchange rate volatility increases the probability of a twist in expectations in the dollar/euro market. Contrary to that in the yen/dollar market there is no impact of volatility on the short-term and long-term expectation formation process. Additionally, Table 3.7 shows the results obtained from a panel probit model (specifications IV to VI) where the exchange rate volatility is regressed on a individual twist-dummy $d_{t,i}$. This individual twist-dummy $d_{t,i}$ is set equal to one ($d_{t,i} = 1$) if the respective forecaster forms destabilizing short-term while stabilizing long-term expectations and is set equal to zero otherwise at the respective point in time. Using the individual expectations of each forecaster the results again indicate that only for the dollar/euro exchange rate an excess volatility increases the probability of twisting behavior. The results for the yen/dollar exchange rate are ambiguous and, however, insignificant. In sum, in the dollar/euro market it is more likely that professional forecasters exhibit a twist in times of excess volatility, whereas in the yen/dollar market no relationship between twist and exchange rate volatility occurs.

Table 3.7: Analysis of exchange rate volatility and twist

Specification	*I*	*II*	*III*	*IV*	*V*	*VI*
Model		Probit			Panel Probit	
Exchange Rate	Yen/Dollar	Dollar/Euro	Yen/Dollar	Yen/Dollar	Dollar/Euro	Yen/Dollar
Period	1989–1998	2003–2007	2003–2007	1989–1998	2003–2007	2003–2007
κ	-.3364	-.8820	-1.309**	-.1609***	-.0860	-.5237***
	(.4015)	(.6451)	(.6352)	(.0605)	(.1078)	(.09112)
λ	-47.82	128.44*	141.75	-6.7206	28.56**	16.95
	(43.79)	(78.96)	(127.23)	(4.3071)	(13.66)	(16.99)
Likelihood Ratio/Wald Chi^2	1.75	4.05	1.37	2.43	4.37	1.00
Prob > Chi^2	.0776	.0441	.2420	.1187	.0365	.3185
Observations	20	10	10	760	500	500

Notes: Table **3.7** shows the estimations results of equation (3.8) $P(d_{t,i} = 1 \mid \lambda_{t,i}) = \kappa_i + \lambda_{t,i}\sigma^2_{(s_t)} + \nu_{t,i}$; *** and * indicate significance at the 1 and 10 percent level, respectively; standard errors are in parentheses.

3.6 Conclusion

In this chapter, we develop and apply consistency restrictions to the dollar/euro and yen/dollar exchange rate forecasts of professional forecasters. We find that short-term forecasts are not consistent with long-term forecasts in the framework of a simple expectation formation process. Moreover, the expectation formation process in the dollar/euro market reveals a behavior referred to as a *twist* which is defined as short-term destabilizing and long-term stabilizing expectations. Considering a more complex expectation formation structure we find that dollar/euro forecasts are internally consistent. However, applying a panel probit analysis we find that this twisting behavior is more likely in periods of excess exchange rate volatility in the dollar/euro market.

In sum, chapters 2 and 3 provide strong evidence that foreign exchange market participants can be regarded as heterogeneous and irrational. More precisely, by accounting for the extrapolative behavior we can distinguish between two groups of foreign market participants, namely stabilizing and destabilizing agents. While the latter group believes in trends in the exchange rate development, stabilizing market participants expect the exchange rate to mean revert to its original level. The subsequent chapter 4 takes this core result into account and develops a market microstructural model which consists of stabilizing and destabilizing actors. Within this microstructural model we show that the central bank can use official intervention to coordinate these groups and effectively influence the exchange rate development.

Chapter 4

The coordination channel of foreign exchange intervention: The Australian case

4.1 Introduction

Official foreign exchange market intervention, defined as sales or purchases of foreign currency by the monetary authorities of a country in order to influence its exchange rate, is typically claimed to affect either the level or the volatility of exchange rates. While belief in the effectiveness of intervention among policy makers is mixed and has shifted over time (Taylor 1994, 1995; Neely 2000, 2006; Schwartz, 2000), empirical results have generally cast serious doubts on the efficacy of sterilized foreign exchange intervention (Sarno and Taylor, 2001). Given that monetary authorities typically take action to sterilize the effects of the resulting change in official foreign assets on the domestic monetary base (Taylor, 1992), the question arises as to how sterilized intervention can affect exchange rates if it does not do so by directly affecting the monetary aggregates.

Traditionally, sterilized intervention is expected to affect exchange rates through one of two channels (Taylor, 1995). If intervention is effective through the first channel, the portfolio balance channel, then the change in the foreign assets of the central bank resulting from the intervention induces private market participants to restructure their international portfolios, thus altering the equilibrium level of the exchange rate. A crucial assumption of the portfolio balance channel is thus that domestic and foreign assets are imperfect substitutes - an assumption which has been rejected repeatedly for major currencies (Lewis, 1999). Moreover, the massive volume of foreign exchange transactions (Bank for International Settlements, 2007) suggests that the typical intervention operation may generate largely insignificant effects on the foreign exchange market (Dominguez and Frankel, 1993; Taylor, 1995).

The effectiveness of intervention via the second channel, the signalling channel, requires that the central bank use foreign exchange interventions to signal future monetary policy to private market agents (Mussa, 1981). A prerequisite of intervention effectiveness via the signalling channel is that interventions are publicly announced. Evidence on the effectiveness of intervention through the signalling channel is mixed (Dominguez and Frankel, 1993; Kaminski and Lewis, 1996).

In a break from reasoning along these traditional lines, analyses based on microstructural models suggest that exchange rate movements may be largely determined by foreign exchange market order flows submitted by heterogeneous market agents, so that intervention becomes a means of disseminating information into the market (Evans and Lyons, 2002; Lyons, 1997). This type of microstructural channel of intervention effectiveness has received some - albeit infrequent and mixed - empirical support (Peiers, 1997; Dominguez, 2003; Neely, 2005). Neely (2006) argues that policy makers may in fact invest some degree of belief in all three transmission channels (portfolio balance, signalling and microstructural).

Within the general class of microstructural models of exchange rate intervention, Taylor (2004, 2005) and Reitz and Taylor (2008a, 2008b) have proposed an alternative transmission channel via which official intervention may be effective: the coordination channel. The reasoning behind the coordination channel is straightforward: if strong and persistent misalignments of the exchange rate are caused by non-fundamental influences, such that a return to equilibrium is hampered by a coordination failure among fundamentals-based traders (Shleifer and Vishny, 1997), then official intervention may act as a coordinating signal, encouraging stabilizing speculators to re-enter the market at the same time.

An immediate problem encountered in attempting to test the coordination channel empirically on recent data is that foreign exchange market intervention has become less common among industrialized countries in recent years. This is not to deny the efficacy of the coordination channel, however, since there is some evidence that the coordinating feature of intervention may in recent years have been captured by policy makers' exchange rate announcements that effectively become 'oral interventions' operating through the coordination channel (Fratzscher, 2006). Nevertheless, the analysis of the efficacy of actual intervention through the coordination channel is clearly hampered by the paucity of recent examples of actual intervention. The continuing intervention activities of the Reserve Bank of Australia (RBA) over the past twenty years thus provides a welcome data base for testing the coordination channel on recent data.

In this chapter, we apply nonlinear econometric modeling techniques in order to investigate the effectiveness of foreign exchange interventions conducted by the RBA in the Australian dollar-US dollar (AUD-USD) market over the period 1984 - 2005, using the microstrucutural framework for the coordination channel developed by Reitz and Taylor (2008a). Our empirical results reveal that the greater the degree of exchange rate misalignment, the weaker becomes informed traders' trading activity. However, official intervention becomes increasingly effective the further the nominal exchange rate deviates from the equilibrium exchange rate, in accordance with the predictions of the coordination channel of intervention effectiveness.

The remainder of the chapter is organized as follows. In section 4.2 we give a brief overview of how the RBA has intervened in the foreign exchange market and we review previous studies focusing on RBA intervention. In section 4.3 we present our microstructural model of intervention. In section 4.4 we develop an empirical model, informed by our theoretical analysis and recent empirical work on nonlinear exchange rate adjustment, while in section 4.5 we describe our daily data set on AUD-USD exchange rates, official intervention and fundamentals. Our main empirical results concerning intervention effectiveness are reported in section 4.6 before the final section concludes.

4.2 The intervention policy and practice of the Reserve Bank of Australia

While the Australian economy can be regarded as relatively small, the Australian dollar (AUD) is the sixth largest currency traded in the world market, and the AUD-USD exchange rate is the fourth heaviest traded currency pair (Bank for International Settlements, 2007). Since the AUD was floated in December 1983, it has moved in a wide range around an average of AUD 1.5 per

USD. Although it adopted a flexible exchange rate regime in the early 1980s, however, the RBA has not become indifferent to exchange rate movements, as reflected in frequent RBA interventions over the ensuing two decades. This intervention policy can be regarded as publicly disclosed in most cases because RBA interventions are generally conducted by entering the broker market directly and announcing the intervention publicly (Edison, Cashin and Liang, 2006). Rogers and Siklos (2003) also note that the RBA regularly announces its intervention operations and communicates its foreign exchange purchases and sales directly to the foreign exchange market. Only occasionally does the RBA use an agent bank to conceal the RBA's presence in the market (Rankin, 1998). Juuttner and Tonkin (1992) emphasize that the Australian market is 'well informed of intervention operations'. Furthermore, the RBA (2003) itself publishes its intervention policy, which has always been one of sterilized intervention. Hutcheson (2003) conducted a questionnaire among exchange rate dealers licensed by the RBA: interestingly, about three quarters of survey participants reported that they believed that there was some degree of credibility in the RBA's intervention effectiveness.

A potential drawback in any empirical analysis of Australian foreign exchange intervention is that the RBA frequently undertakes operations in both securities and foreign exchange on behalf of the Australian government. Each day, the government is required to make payments as part of its regular operations, reflecting payments for foreign goods and services or expenses involved in maintaining embassies. To ensure that these transactions do not affect the level of reserves in the RBA portfolio, the RBA buys or sells foreign exchange. These operations are carried out at market prices. For the period 1989 to 2005, the total sales of foreign exchange to the government were around AUD 4 billion per financial year (RBA 2004, p.11), while trades with other market participants were on average AUD 3 billion per financial year. Although trades with the government have become less important in recent years they are still quite substantial (Edison, Cashin and Liang, 2006). However, transactions with the government can be to some extent regarded as intervention policy if the RBA considers these transaction when they are passed through as destabilizing for the market. In that case the government's needs are met from the RBA portfolio, and are passed through with a time lag to the market when market conditions are more favourable (RBA 2000, p.12). This feature may therefore confound an analysis of official intervention since the RBA purchases domestic or foreign currency not only to influence the exchange rate, but also to meet the government's demand for and supply of foreign currency. While this may to some extent explain the mixed findings of studies of Australian intervention effectiveness - as discussed below - it also suggests that if a statistically significant influence of RBA intervention on exchange rates can be detected even given this feature of the market, then this would provide strong evidence of effectiveness.

An advantage of analyzing the AUD-USD market in this context, however, arises from the fact that the US monetary authorities have refrained from intervening in the AUD-USD market (Federal Reserve Bank, 2006). Therefore, we can conclude that, insofar as there is a significant link between intervention and the exchange rate, it arises from RBA intervention.

Our data span the sample period from January 1984 to March 2005, and includes the temporary excess volatility due to the 1997 - 98 Asian economic crisis and the 1998 - 99 Russian financial crisis, both of which led to large-scale interventions by the RBA (see Figure 4.1). Over our sample period, RBA intervention operations took place on 2,224 out of a total of 5,542 trading days (40.1 percent). Thus, the RBA intervened heavily compared to other central banks (Kearns and Rigobon, 2005). Neely (2000) reports that, over nearly the same period, fourteen central banks intervened on average on only about 4 - 5 percent of all trading days. The average size of intervention was USD 40 million - compared to a daily traded turnover in the AUD of USD 72 billion (Rankin, 1998) - with the largest intervention being a dollar sale of USD 898 million in August 1992. The total amount of US dollars bought in intervention operations over our sample period exceeded USD 29 billion. After a long period of frequent intervention operations until the early 1990s, the RBA refrained from intervening in the foreign exchange market during the mid 1990s and changed its intervention strategy, moving from generally small daily interventions with frequent changes in direction to less frequent but larger scale interventions. During the whole period from 1983 to 2005 a reserves position of AUD 19 billion was built up, mostly originating from the period between 1988 and 1992.

Since the RBA publishes its intervention data series it is readily available and, therefore, frequently used in order to examine the intervention policy of the RBA. Applying Friedman's (1953) profitability test[1] for intervention effectiveness, Andrew and Broadbent (1994) estimate profits of AUD 3.4 billion for the RBA in the period from December 1983 to June 1994, suggesting that its foreign exchange operations were stabilizing for the AUD as the RBA bought foreign exchange when its price was low and sold it when its price was high. Using the same profitability measure, Becker and Sinclair

[1] The application of this test relies on the assumption that the central bank acts as a stabilizing speculator, buying (selling) the foreign currency when the price is low (high) and, therefore, realizing profits by contemporaneously mitigating the exchange rate volatility.

(2004) lengthen the sample period and estimate profits of AUD 5.8 billion for the RBA for the period from December 1983 to June 2004. Hence, both of these studies conclude that RBA interventions exerted a stabilizing influence on the AUD-USD exchange rate. Additionally, Kearns and Rigobon (2005) support the view that over the period from 1986 to 1993, RBA interventions contemporaneously affected the exchange rate level significantly.[2] Moreover, Kearns and Rigobon (2005) identify the intervention strategy as primarily one of slowing down otherwise precipitous exchange rate movements or 'leaning against the wind', as also suggested by a number of previous studies (Rogers and Siklos, 2003; Kim and Sheen, 2002; McKenzie, 2004). Hopkins and Murphy (1997) undertake a case study approach covering the period of July to October 1993 where the AUD experienced a high depreciation. They find that interventions and associated statements by the RBA did enhance the stability of the market. In contrast, Makin and Shaw (1997) conclude that neither the exchange rate level nor exchange rate volatility was influenced by RBA interventions during 1983 and 1993. In recent work, Rogers and Siklos (2003) lengthen the sample period and support this finding: they find little evidence that the RBA was successful in managing the AUD exchange rate during 1983 to 1997. In particular, their results suggest that RBA interventions were largely ineffective in affecting the level of the exchange rate although the volatility and kurtosis of AUD-USD exchange rate movements were modestly affected.

According to Edison, Cashin and Liang (2006), who use an event-study technique, the foreign exchange operations of the RBA during 1984 to 2001 did not consistently influence the level of the AUD-USD. However, they find some indication of a 'leaning against the wind' intervention strategy in the way that on days when RBA purchased AUD, the currency often strengthened either immediately or over time by reversing a previously depreciating trend. Additionally, these authors found that RBA interventions generally tended to increase exchange rate volatility, suggesting that they contributed to market uncertainty. Edison, Cashin and Liang (2006) therefore conclude that RBA intervention could not be regarded as being effective in general. This conclusion is also supported by Ahdi, Ahmed and Abdelwahed (2003), who apply a fractionally integrated generalized autoregressive conditional heteroskedasticity (FIGARCH) model and conclude that RBA intervention usually increases exchange rate volatility.

In contrast to the mixed results concerning the effectiveness of in-

[2]This view is also supported by the evidence reported by Karunaratne (1996) and Kim, Kortian and Sheen (2000) and, more recently, by Kim and Pham (2006).

tervention, a much clearer picture arises from the extensive research on the *motives* for central bank intervention. Kim and Sheen (2002), for example, provide evidence that the probability of RBA intervention is significantly higher in periods of deviations of the exchange rate from its trend level. This in itself provides at least prima facie support for the existence of a coordination channel of intervention. For the coordination channel to be effective, however, we also need to demonstrate that intervention tends to be more effective the greater is the degree of misalignment of the exchange rate, and that is one purpose of the research reported in this chapter.

Overall, we would argue that the mixed evidence on the effectiveness of foreign exchange market intervention by the RBA may be due to two related features of previous analyses. First, previous studies have used the traditional taxonomy of the portfolio balance and signalling channels of intervention effectiveness, whereas we believe that RBA intervention may have largely operated through the coordination channel. Second, the coordination channel implies a subtle nonlinearity in intervention effectiveness that will not have been captured within the linear framework of traditional empirical analysis.

4.3 A microstructural model of the coordination channel of intervention effectiveness

There is a substantial literature on the effectiveness of foreign exchange intervention (Sarno and Taylor, 2001). While traditional studies focus on the portfolio or signalling channel, more recently market microstructural approaches have become popular in examining the effect of foreign exchange market intervention (e.g. Dominguez, 2003). Our model belongs to the latter group and follows the framework developed by Reitz and Taylor (2008a).

Assuming that exchange rates are determined in an order-driven market governed by heterogeneous agents (De Grauwe and Grimaldi 2005, 2006), the exchange rate change at time $t+1$ can be expressed as a function of net order flows from informed and uninformed trades plus a noise term:

$$s_{t+1} = s_t + a^M(D_t^I + D_t^U) + \epsilon_{t+1}, \tag{4.1}$$

where s_t is the logarithm of the spot exchange rate at time t, defined as AUD per US dollar, and a^M is a positive reaction coefficient determined by the market maker. D_t^I and D_t^U denote the net order flow from informed and uninformed speculators, respectively. The exchange rate change depends on the net order flow from both informed and uninformed speculators, because the market maker does not observe them individually.

Orders are submitted by risk-neutral speculators and depend on expected excess returns, which consist of the expected change in the exchange rate and the interest differential. Assuming that uninformed traders correspond to chartists or technical traders (Menkhoff and Taylor, 2007), we follow Reitz and Taylor (2008) and model the uninformed trader's order as a positive function of the recent return, plus a term in the interest differential:

$$D_t^U = a^U(s_t - s_{t-1}) + b^U(i_t^* - i_t), \tag{4.2}$$

where i_t^* and i_t represent the interest rate of foreign and home currency deposits, respectively. While the parameter a^U is expected to be positive, the expected sign of b^U is not immediately clear. According to the uncovered interest rate parity (UIP) condition, the interest differential $(i_t^* - i_t)$ should be an unbiased predictor of the percentage change in the exchange rate. Equivalently, given that covered interest rate parity is known to hold closely, at least among eurodeposit interest rates (Taylor, 1987, 1989), UIP implies that the forward exchange rate should be an unbiased predictor of the spot rate. If uninformed traders believe in UIP, therefore, one would expect b^U to be positive. However, the failure of UIP (equivalently, the failure of forward rate unbiasedness) is so well documented as to have established itself as a stylized fact (Froot and Thaler, 1990; Taylor, 1995), and it seems that, if anything, there is a tendency among traders to bet against UIP using various 'forward-rate bias' or 'carry trade' strategies (Fabozzi, 2001; Rosenberg, 2003; Galati, Heath and McGuire, 2007), which would suggest a negative sign for b^U.[3] Overall, therefore, the sign of this coefficient is ambiguous.

Compared to uninformed traders, informed traders base their expectations considering future exchange rate development on an analysis of exchange rate fundamentals, based on their view of a time-varying long-term fundamental equilibrium value, denoted f_t. While the exchange rate is expected to revert towards f_t over time, the weight attached to the deviation from fundamentals in determining orders may vary over time. Thus, informed traders' orders may be expressed as:

$$D_t^I = a^I w_t(f_t - s_t) + b^I(i_t^* - i_t), \tag{4.3}$$

[3] The act of buying high-interest rate currencies is also referred to as a 'carry trade' (Galati and Melvin, 2004).

where a^I is a positive reaction function coefficient and w_t determines the confidence of informed speculators in fundamental analysis. Again, following similar reasoning as in the case of the uninformed speculator parameter b^U, the sign of the coefficient on the interest differential in (4.3), b^I, is ambiguous.

According to equation (4.3), as long as $w_t > 0$, orders of informed traders contribute to stabilizing speculation in the sense that they will tend to drive the exchange rate toward its equilibrium value. The confidence measure w_t is at the center of our analysis, because it reflects the time-varying impact of stabilizing speculation on exchange rates thereby providing the basis for the coordination channel of intervention effectiveness. We assume that informed traders' confidence in the fundamentals can be expressed as a function of the standardized absolute misalignment and the intervention of the central bank:

$$c_t = -(\phi_1 - \phi_2 INT_t)\frac{|f_t - s_t|}{\sigma_t^S} \tag{4.4}$$

and

$$w_t = \frac{2exp(c_t)}{1 + exp(c_t)} \tag{4.5}$$

and where σ_t^S denotes the conditional standard deviation of exchange rate movements. If the distance between the actual exchange rate and its fundamental value increases, fundamental analysis wrongly predicts the sign of the exchange rate change, causing informed traders to refrain from submitting orders (Shleifer and Vishny, 1997). On the other hand, if the degree of misalignments falls so that fundamental analysis correctly predicts exchange rate movements, this encouraged informed traders to submit orders based on fundamental analysis. Hence, it seems reasonable to postulate that a standardized measure of absolute misalignment should influence traders' confidence in fundamentals. Moreover - and crucial to the framework of the coordination channel - we allow the trading activity of central banks in the foreign exchange market to influence informed traders' confidence in fundamental analysis. If the monetary authority sells an overvalued currency, it reveals its commitment to a lower exchange rate. In the market microstructure literature, central banks are regarded to have superior information about the exchange rate, because they observe innovations in fundamental data series in advance and are able to assess their impact on future exchange rate returns (Sager and Taylor, 2006). Hence, informed traders become more confident that the exchange rate will revert to its fundamental value and engage in trading. The market increasingly focuses on fundamentals, so interventions may be regarded as a device with which to coordinate traders' expectations.

As argued by Taylor (2004, 2005) and Reitz and Taylor (2008), the influence of intervention operations on traders' confidence through the coordination channel should depend on the level of current misalignment. In the neighborhood of the fundamental value, the potential stabilizing gains of intervention will be negligible because informed traders will interpret small misalignments as temporary phenomena exploitable for speculative purposes and will trade intensively in the market. If the misalignment is large, however, intervention will tend to be more effective, because informed traders - who have reduced their orders because of a loss in confidence in the fundamentals - may now be encouraged to re-enter the market by the central bank intervention. Finally, it must be noted that the purchase of an overvalued currency by the monetary authority would puzzle informed traders and perhaps drive them out of the market. To capture these misleading signals, we set an indicator variable equal to -1 if the exchange rate is overvalued and equal to $+1$ if it is undervalued according to the measure of the fundamental equilibrium. Multiplying the indicator variable by the current sale or purchase provides us with an intervention measure (INT_t) that is positive only if the central bank operates in the appropriate direction. A logistic normalization transforms the value c_t into a confidence measure w_t.[4] Combining equations (4.1) - (4.5), the solution for the exchange rates can then be derived as:

$$s_{t+1} = s_t + \alpha(s_t - s_{t-1}) + \delta w_t(f_t - s_t) + \gamma(i_t^* - i_t) + \epsilon_{t+1}, \tag{4.6}$$

with $\alpha = a^M a^U > 0$, $\delta = a^M a^I > 0$ and $\gamma = a^M(b^U + b^I)$ (the sign of γ being ambiguous).

From equation (4.6) we can see that, for a given value of δ, informed traders' stabilizing impact on the exchange rate increases nonlinearly with their confidence in fundamental analysis. If, for instance, the exchange rate is near its fundamental equilibrium value, informed traders provide maximum mean reversion, since w_t will be close to unity. However, as the exchange rate becomes increasingly misaligned, informed traders reduce their orders and mean reversion weakens. This creates a role for central bank intervention that, through its coordinating influence on informed traders, effectively raises their confidence in the fundamentals and generates an increase in the degree

[4]With the logistic form of equation (4.4) we follow the switching mechanism of Brock and Hommes (1997) and Lux (1998) and is the spirit of recent work by De Grauwe and Grimaldi (2005, 2006), who develop a similar switching function in their model of chartist-fundamentalist interaction.

of mean reversion of the nominal exchange rate towards the fundamental equilibrium. We now turn to the empirical implementation of the model.

4.4 The empirical model

Our aim is to investigate empirically the role of RBA intervention through an investigation of the nonlinear theoretical exchange rate model outlined in the previous section. Our empirical model belongs to the STR (Smooth Transition Regression) family of models originally proposed by Ozaki (1985) and further developed and analyzed by Teräsvirta and Anderson (1992), Granger and Teräsvirta (1993) and Teräsvirta (1994). STR models allow an economic variable to follow a given number of regimes with switches between regimes achieved in a smooth and continuous fashion and governed by the value of a particular variable or group of variables. The STR framework has previously proved successful in applications to exchange rate behaviour (Taylor and Peel, 2000; Taylor, Peel and Sarno, 2001; Kilian and Taylor, 2003).[5]

In order to examine the empirical evidence of market microstructure model we use daily data, implying that the conditional variance of exchange rate returns cannot be treated as constant over time. To cope with the heteroskedastic properties of daily exchange rate returns, we therefore apply the STR-GARCH procedure originally developed by Lundbergh and Teräsvirta (1998) and applied by Gallagher and Taylor (2001) and Reitz and Westerhoff (2003). The STR-GARCH model consists of a mean equation containing a smooth transition function and a standard GARCH(1,1) volatility equation. In the present context, given the theoretical model outlined above, this suggests an empirical model of the form:

$$\Delta s_t = \alpha \Delta s_{t-1} + \delta w_t (f_{t-1} - s_{t-1}) + \gamma (i^*_{t-1} - i_{t-1}) + \epsilon_t \tag{4.7}$$

$$w_t(\phi, f_{t-d}, int_{t-d}, h_{t-d}) = \frac{2exp(-(\phi_1 - \phi_2 INT_{t-1})\frac{|f_{t-d}-s_{t-d}|}{\sqrt{h_{t-d}}})}{1 + exp(-(\phi_1 - \phi_2 INT_{t-1})\frac{|f_{t-d}-s_{t-d}|}{\sqrt{h_{t-d}}})} \tag{4.8}$$

$$h_t = \beta_0 + \beta_1 \epsilon^2_{t-1} + \beta_2 h_{t-1}, \tag{4.9}$$

[5]De Grauwe and Grimaldi (2001) apply a quadratic specification to model deviations of the exchange rate from fundamental equilibrium, which can be interpreted as an approximation to a STAR specification.

where Δ is the first-difference operator, INT_t denotes net purchases of US dollars against Australian dollars, and $\epsilon = \nu_t\sqrt{h_t}$ and ν_t^{iid} is N(0,1). There are two major differences between the empirical model (4.7) - (4.9) and the theoretical model set out in the previous section. First, we introduce a GARCH model to capture the conditional variance of the error term, which is important given that we apply our model to daily exchange rate movements. Second, we allow in our empirical model for a value of the delay parameter, d, different from one since the importance of searching for an appropriate value of the delay parameter in empirical applications of STR models has been stressed by Teräsvirta and others (e.g. Teräsvirta and Anderson, 1992; Granger and Teräsvirta, 1993: Teräsvirta, 1994).

4.5 The data

The exchange rate data used in this study are daily interbank mid-rate quotations (10.00am Sydney) of the spot AUD exchange rates against the US dollar. The price of one US dollar is expressed in AUD. In terms of the preceding analysis, therefore, Australia represents the home economy while the US is taken as the foreign economy. The home interest rate is thus i^{AUS}, the overnight AUD deposit interest rate (10.00am Sydney), and the foreign interest rate is i^{USD}, the overnight US dollar deposit interest rate. The intervention data was kindly provided by the RBA, while the exchange and interest rates are taken from Datastream.

All series are daily frequency, and cover the period January 2, 1984 to March 29, 2005 (5,542 trading day observations). We assume that the fundamental equilibrium value of the exchange rate, f_t, can be adequately described by the purchasing power parity (ppp) level, based on relative consumer prices. Takagi (1991) provides evidence from survey data that foreign exchange market participants accept ppp as the long-term exchange rate equilibrium. Monthly observations of the consumer price indices (CPIs) were taken from the International Monetary Fund's International Financial Statistics database to construct a measure of the ppp fundamental as $f_t = log(CPI_t^{USD}) - log(CPI_t^{AUD})$.[6] Daily exchange rates, the ppp fundamental and the RBA intervention record are presented in Figure 4.1.

[6]The sample mean of this series was removed prior to the empirical analysis.

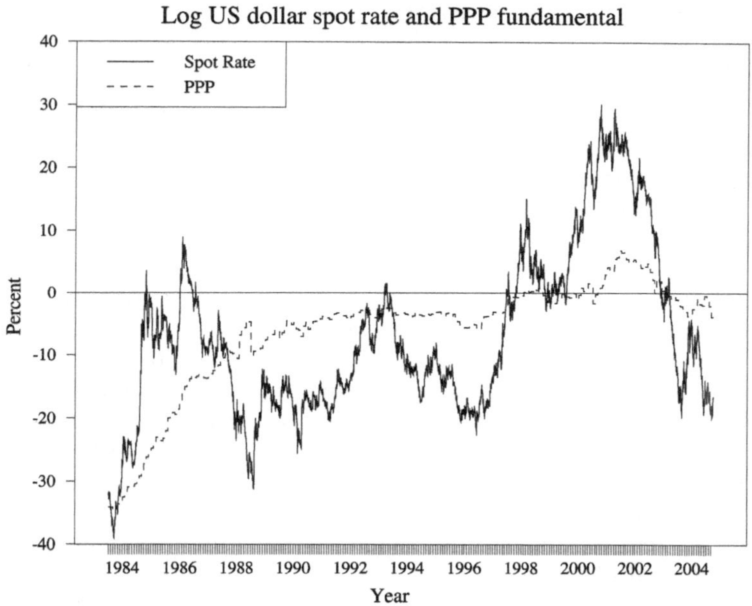

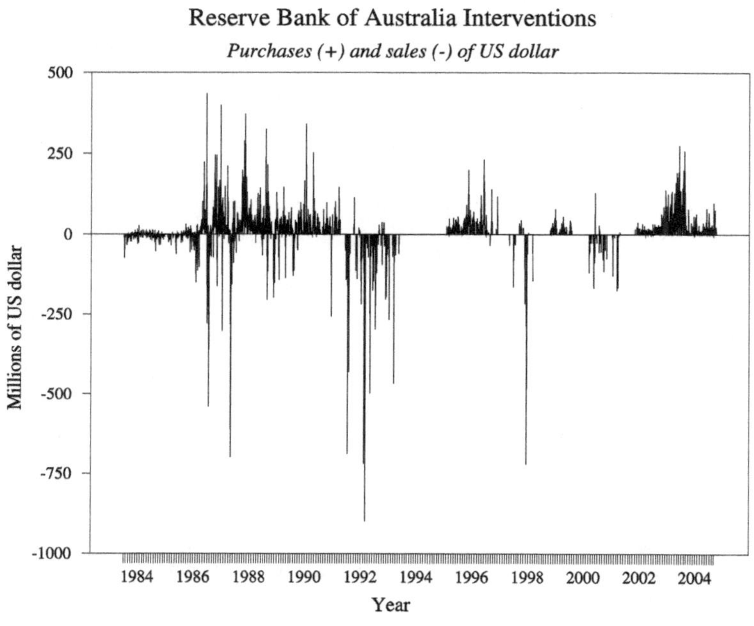

Figure 4.1: Log US dollar spot rate, PPP fundamental, and RBA intervention

4.6 Estimation results

The modeling procedure for building STR models was carried out as suggested by Granger and Teräsvirta (1993) and Teräsvirta (1994). First, linear autoregressive models were estimated in order to choose the lag order of the autoregressive term on the basis of the Bayes Information Criterion criterion. As Table 4.1 indicates, we found that first-order autocorrelation seemed to be appropriate for exchange rate returns in our data. Second, we tested linearity against the STR model for different values of the delay parameter d, using the linear model ($w_t = 1$, for all t) as the null hypothesis and choosing the value of d that gives the smallest marginal significance level.[7] The transition parameters ϕ_1 and ϕ_2 are slope parameters that determine the speed of transition between the two extreme regimes, with low absolute values resulting in slower transition. Since (4.8) is a linear transformation of the standard logistic transition function as proposed by Teräsvirta and Anderson (1992), robust standard errors may be derived. This is important because conditional normality cannot be maintained. Under fairly weak regularity conditions, however, the resulting robust estimates are consistent even when the conditional distribution of the residuals is non-normal (Bollerslev and Wooldridge, 1992). Teräsvirta (1994) points out that estimating the transition parameters may cause particular problems such as slow convergence of the estimation routine or overestimation, and suggests setting the initial value of the transition parameters equal to the reciprocal of the sample variance of the transition variable in the iterative estimation procedure. However, the recommended rescaling of the transition variable by means of the conditional standard deviation has already been introduced for theoretical reasons. On the basis of this standardization, we therefore set $\phi_1 = 1$ and $\phi_2 = 0$ as the starting values for the estimation routine. Table 4.1 contains our final estimation results.

The estimation results are pleasing in the sense that the point estimates of the coefficients are significantly different from zero (except for α) and appropriately signed and the estimated model passes a number of diagnostic checks for remaining serial correlation, nonlinearity or conditional heteroscedasticity in the standardized residuals. We also tested the model against a restricted model in which $\delta = \gamma = \phi_1 = \phi_2 = 0$, so that the constrained model became a simple AR(1)-GARCH(1,1) model. The resulting test statistic, *LRT*, is reported in Table 4.1, and reveals that the simple

[7] Checking the standardized residuals of the model reveals that setting $d = 4$ passes the test for no remaining nonlinearity up to ten lags using the specification test of Eitrheim and Teräsvirta (1996).

Table 4.1: Parameter estimates of the STR GARCH model

	January 2, 1984 - March 29, 2005
γ	$-1.47(2.08)^{**}$
α	0.01 (0.91)
δ	$0.02(3.12)^{***}$
ϕ_1	$-0.268(2.83)^{***}$
ϕ_2	$0.003(3.01)^{***}$
β_0	$0.005(3.59)^{***}$
β_1	$0.066(7.03)^{***}$
β_2	$0.925(89.15)^{***}$
LLh	107.5
LRT	32.16^{***}
$AR(1)$	0.32
$AR(5)$	0.24
$ARCH(1)$	0.21
$ARCH(5)$	0.55
$NRNL$	0.17

Notes: The sample contains daily observations of the dollar spot exchange rate against the Australian dollar from January 1984 to March 2005. α, δ, γ, ϕ indicate the estimated parameters of the mean equations, β_0, β_1, and β_2 are the estimated GARCH(1,1) parameters, LLh is the log likelihood value, LRT is the likelihood ratio test statistic with restrictions $\alpha = \delta = \gamma = \phi = 0$. $AR(p)$ denotes the p-value for the Ljung-Box statistic for serial correlation of the residuals up to p lags. $ARCH(q)$ denotes the p-value for the Ljung-Box statistic for serial correlation of the standardized squared residuals up to q lags. $NRNL$ is the lowest p-value for no remaining nonlinearity up to ten lags. t-statistics in parentheses are based on robust estimates of the covariance matrices of the parameter estimates. *(**,***) denotes significance at the 10 (5, 1) percent level.

AR(1)-GARCH(1,1) model is rejected against our STR-GARCH model at the one percent significance level.

While the positive signs of the point estimates of the trader coefficients, i.e. α and δ respectively, accord with our theoretical priors, only the estimate of the informed trader δ coefficient is statistically significant. The fact that the estimate of the uninformed trader coefficient α is statistically insignificant at the five percent level reveals that assuming a simple trend-following trading strategy may not be sufficient in order to model the average influence of chartist behavior (Menkhoff and Taylor, 2007). On the other hand, a negative and statistically significant point estimate of the interest rate differential coefficient γ implies, on average, an appreciation of the AUD when Australian interest rates are higher than US interest rates. Given our discussion of the likely sign of the coefficients b^U and b^I in section 4.3, however, this is not surprising and is consistent with evidence on the prevalence of so-called 'carry trade' (Galati, Heath and McGuire, 2007).

The statistically significant point estimate of ϕ_1 indicates a high speed of transition between regimes with respect to the standardized misalignment. The interpretation in terms of the model is straightforward. If the exchange rate converges towards the ppp value - as predicted by fundamental analysis—informed traders gain confidence in fundamental analysis and trade more heavily in the market. But, the more the exchange rate deviates from ppp, the more reluctant are informed traders to submit stabilizing orders. However, the statistically significant and positive point estimate of the intervention parameter ϕ_2 indicates that an RBA intervention operation was able to compensate for the lack of confidence caused by exchange rate misalignment. The coefficient point estimates suggest that, at the average level of exchange volatility, a 10 percent misalignment results in a daily mean reversion towards fundamentals of 0.046 percent, or of 11.57 percent on an annualized basis. Under these circumstances an intervention of USD 50 million increases the mean reversion parameter to 0.6 percent. The degree of mean reversion induced by a slightly larger than average intervention operation is therefore some ten times higher with the intervention than without it, indicating an economically significant contribution to market stability from the RBA. From the model's perspective, the implication is that RBA interventions encouraged agents to engage in fundamental speculation, thereby helping to bring the exchange rate back towards the ppp level. Overall, our estimation results provide evidence for the idea that RBA interventions exhibit a stabilizing influence on the AUD-USD exchange rate by coordinating stabilizing speculation based on exchanger rate fundamentals.

Within the coordination channel, intervention operations alter the composition of the foreign exchange market, implying that the effect of intervention on exchange rates is presumed to be persistent. However, it might be argued that the record of frequent RBA operations introduced some habit persistence and may have led informed traders to return to the foreign exchange market only if the central bank persistently intervenes. Put differently, stopping operations may be interpreted as an adverse signal thereby thwarting the stabilizing effect of recent intervention. On the other hand, Neely (2005) points out that there is good reason to assume that the overall effect of intervention on exchange rates 'takes at least a few days'. To assess the persistence of intervention effectiveness, we therefore allow for additional lags in the transition function. The estimation routine reveals that lag orders higher than four are statistically insignificant at the ten percent level implying that the inclusion of the last four operations seems to be sufficient. The

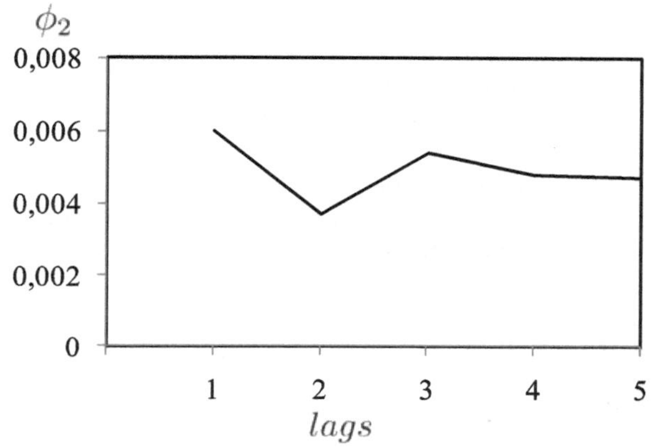

Figure 4.2: Cumulative value of impact coefficient of intervention on traders' confidence

cumulative influence of intervention on exchange rates via the coordination channel is represented in Figure 4.2.

The cumulative coefficients reveal that the influence of intervention on traders' confidence drops slightly at the next trading day and then recovers. Obviously, it takes time to develop the total influence of intervention on exchange rates via the coordination channel. This corresponds to Neely's (2005) conjecture that the entire effect of intervention on exchange rates is felt over a few days. In general, however, the inclusion of additional lags confirms the persistence of intervention effectiveness via the coordination channel.

4.7 Conclusion

In contrast to the standard linear time-series approaches employed by a number of previous contributions on RBA intervention effectiveness, this chapter focuses on the RBA's potential to influence exchange rates in a nonlinear fashion. We estimated a microstructural model of daily exchange rate behavior in order to study the effectiveness of RBA interventions in the AUD-USD foreign exchange market and in particular to examine the relevance of the coordination channel of intervention effectiveness. Within our model, mean reversion of the exchange rate is provided by stabilizing speculation of informed traders, yet their foreign exchange market activity depends on their confidence in fundamental analysis. Our model estimates suggest that the further removed the exchange rate is from the underlying fundamental value, the weaker becomes informed traders' activity. This nonlinearity provides the basis for the coordinating role of central bank intervention. According to the coordination channel, intervention operations may stabilize exchange rates by coordinating the actions of informed traders. In our analysis, the fundamental value of the exchange rate was approximated by a measure of purchasing power parity, implying that intervention effectiveness is assessed by testing whether intervention operations tend to induce stability in the real exchange rate. In line with the results of Taylor (2004, 2005), our empirical analysis provides evidence in favor of this route of intervention effectiveness. In particular, it was shown that the RBA's intervention policy tended to reduce misalignments of the AUD-USD exchange rate in a manner consistent with the coordination channel. Moreover, the inclusion of additional lags in the confidence function confirms the persistence of intervention effectiveness via the coordination channel.

Overall, we can draw the following conclusions from our research. First, our work provides evidence that RBA interventions affected the AUD-USD exchange rate in a nonlinear fashion over the sample period and significantly increased the degree of exchange rate stability. More particularly, our results suggest that intervention will tend to be more effective the greater is the degree of misalignment and provide strong evidence that RBA interventions tend to work through the coordination channel. Since this channel of intervention effectiveness is predicated on the assumption that the relationship between exchange rates and interventions is nonlinear one, we are also able to suggest why previous studies may not have been successful in evaluating the effectiveness of RBA interventions. Moreover, our results explain why the RBA continued to intervene in the foreign exchange market. In sum, Chapter 4 provides evidence for the effectiveness of central bank intervention in the foreign exchange market. The subsequent chapter 5 resumes the discussion on the effectiveness of the central banks policy. However, chapter 5 focuses on the money market and changes the perspective away from the central bank towards the financial market. Put differently, chapter 5 investigates whether the financial market expects the G7 central banks to rule out monetary policy by the means of a specific monetary policy rule, namely the Taylor rule.

Chapter 5

Ex-Ante Taylor rules – Evidence from the G7 countries

5.1 Introduction

In his seminal paper John B. Taylor (1993) explains the development of the U.S. prime rate in terms of a monetary policy reaction function of the Federal Reserve Bank (Fed). The Fed sets the short-term interest rate in accordance with an equilibrium rate from which it deviates whenever actual inflation and/or actual output deviate from target levels. The so-called Taylor rule has been extended in several ways especially by taking into account the forward-looking behavior of central banks and their intention to smooth the interest rate adjustment. Such Taylor-type rules have gained significant importance in both monetary theory and policy. Although the structure of Taylor-type rules is simple, it captures the essence of the behavior of the monetary authority. Probably due to this feature, the application of Taylor-type rules for describing central bank behavior is not only limited to the academic community. Applications can also be found in various publications of the financial industry when commercial banks and others intend to describe and forecast central bank behavior.

As the pioneers of the application of Taylor rules, Clarida et al. (1998) find that the monetary policy of the G7 central banks is Taylor-rule based. Both papers, i.e., Taylor (1993) and Clarida et al. (1998), had a substantial impact on the field of applied monetary policy. In this chapter we use the Consensus Economic Forecast (CEF) poll which includes interest rate, real output growth and inflation rate forecasts for the G7 countries and allows us to analyze two fundamental questions that relate the financial market to the Taylor rule. First, we can investigate in general whether professional forecasters believe in such Taylor-type rules. Second, as the poll started in 1989 we are able to test whether the financial market already applied Taylor-type rules in advance to the publications of Taylor (1993) and Clarida et al. (1998). Since the Taylor-type rules state that output, inflation and the interest rate are linked through a certain relationship, it is possible to check whether the forecasts are internally consistent (i.e., display relationships known from estimation of Taylor-type rules) or whether they are inconsistent in a sense that financial market participants talk a lot about Taylor rules when describing the observed behavior of a central bank but do not employ this reasoning in their forecasts of the interest rate, the inflation rate, and output changes.

In this chapter we change the perspective of looking at interest rate rules from the typical use in the academic literature as a reaction function explaining central bank behavior to the discussion of 'rules versus discretion'. We analyze whether, in the perception of financial markets, the G7 central banks are assumed to be rule-based. In order to do so, the chapter is structured as follows: The subsequent section 5.2 sets out the concept of Taylor-type rules and briefly presents the core results that have emerged from the respective empirical literature. Section 5.3 describes the data employed. Section 5.4 presents the regressions and main results for the full sample while section 5.5 investigates the time period prior to the Taylor rule literature. Finally, section 5.6 concludes.

5.2 The morphology of Taylor-type rules

Since the seminal paper of Taylor (1993), it has virtually become conventional to describe the interest rate setting behavior of central banks in terms of monetary policy reaction functions. In its plain form, the so-called Taylor rule states that the short-term interest rate which, in this analysis, represents the instrument of a central bank reacts to deviations of inflation and output from their respective targets. Clarida et al. (1998) proposed a forward-looking variant of the Taylor rule which takes into account the pre-emptive nature of monetary policy as well as an interest smoothing behavior of central banks. This particular type of reaction function has become very popular in applied empirical research on Taylor rules but are still in the spirit of the Taylor rule. Formulations of this type represent a modification of the original Taylor rule. Therefore, the literature often refers to them as Taylor-type rules.

A number of studies demonstrate that the Fed's monetary policy can be explained by this kind of reaction functions. The most prominent studies are Taylor (1999), Judd and Rudebusch (1998) and Clarida et al. (2000). While Taylor (1999) examines the fit of the original Taylor rule, Judd and Rudebusch (1998) incorporate interest rate smoothing in a modified version. Finally, Clarida et al. (2000) introduced forward-looking elements. All authors demonstrate that the monetary policy of the Fed can reasonably well be explained by Taylor-type rules.[1]

Following Clarida et al. (1998, 2000) the baseline forward-looking policy rule takes the form:

$$i_t^* = \bar{i} + \alpha_1 E_t(\pi_{t+k} - \pi^*) + \alpha_2 E_t(y_{t+q} - y_{t+q}^*), \tag{5.1}$$

where i^* is the desired level of the nominal short-term interest rate, and $\bar{i}$ is its equilibrium level. The second term on the right-hand side is the expected deviation of the k-period ahead inflation rate (π) from the target rate (π^*) which is assumed to be constant over time. The third term is the expected deviation of the q-period ahead level of output (y) from its natural level (y^*) (i.e., the output gap). The coefficients α_1 and α_2 represent the intensity with which the desired interest rate of the central bank reacts to the inflation and the output gap.The assumption of interest rate smoothing behavior then leads to

$$i_t = (1 - \rho)i_t^* + \rho i_{t-1} + \nu_t, \tag{5.2}$$

where the parameter ρ (with $0 < \rho < 1$) describes the degree of interest rate smoothing and ν_t represents an i.i.d. exogenous random shock to the interest rate. Combining (5.1) and (5.2) leads to:

$$i_t = (1 - \rho)(\bar{i} + \alpha_1 E_t(\pi_{t+k} - \pi^*) + \alpha_2 E_t(y_{t+q} - y_{t+q}^*)) + \rho i_{t-1} + \nu_t \tag{5.3}$$

Equation (5.3) represents the econometric specification which is commonly used to describe the central bank behavior. Since the right-hand side of equation (5.3) includes expectations that are not directly observable it is common to substitute them by the observed ex-post levels of the respective variables and rearrange the estimation equation into a form that contains the expectation errors of the central bank in the error term. This form is then estimated based on the General Methods of Moments. Equation (5.3) becomes the plain Taylor rule when ρ is assumed to be zero and the horizons

[1] See Hamalainen (2004) for a survey of empirical studies related to the US.

of the forward-looking behavior of the central bank, k and q, are set equal to zero.

The main message generated by empirical studies focusing on the G7 central banks can be summarized as follows. First, forward-looking specifications seem to fit the central bank's behavior better than contemporaneous versions. Here the forward-looking feature is most relevant for the inflation gap with the horizon (k) being about one year. Second, the relevance of the Taylor principle for stability, i.e. a reaction coefficient for inflation being greater than unity, is well demonstrated and its presence is a strong feature of the more recent monetary policy. Third, the reaction coefficient for the output gap is mostly significant but has a significant lower level compared to the inflation gap coefficient.[2] Fourth, persistence in the prime rate is a strong feature in the data. However, it is not yet clear whether this is due to intended interest rate smoothing by the central bank or whether it is due to a strong autocorrelation in the shocks upon which monetary policy reacts.[3]

Our analysis takes the afore-mentioned four core results of Taylor-type rules as its starting point and interprets them as (historical) information on the central bank's behavior that is available for financial market participants. If the latter believe in the Taylor-type rules, we would expect to observe this in their simultaneous forecasts of the short-term interest rate, the inflation rate and output changes. In this case, the forecasts of the three variables can hardly be independent of each other. They rather should display the same links and dependencies that the estimated reaction functions suggest. We therefore estimate variants of equation (5.3) based on reported forecasts of financial market participants to answer the question that is raised in the title. Before we present the results in section 5.4 and 5.5, the subsequent section 5.3 briefly introduces our data set.

5.3 Survey studies and data

In this chapter we use survey data from the Consensus Economic Forecast (CEF) poll. This survey regularly asks professional forecasters about their projection of several financial and real economy variables such as interest

[2]In particular, for the output gap the literature demonstrated that it is relevant to discriminate between ex post and real-time data (Orphanides, 2001).

[3]Since this issue is also not of a strong concern in the present chapter we refer to the recent literature. See, for instance, Rudebusch (2006).

rates, unemployment rates and GDP growth. The data set has several advantages over other surveys and is, thus, less subject to some of the weaknesses often associated with survey data. First, the individual forecasts are published together with the names of the forecasters' company. As this allows everybody to evaluate the performance of the company, the goodness of the forecasts can be expected to have an effect on the reputation of the forecasters.[4] This is expected to increase the incentives of the survey participants to submit their best rather than their strategic forecast (see Keane and Runkle 1990).[5] Second, unlike some other surveys, forecasters participating in the CEF poll do not only submit the direction of the expected change of the macroeconomic variable, but forecast a specific level which allows for more differentiation between individual forecasts. Third, the survey data are readily available to the public so that our results can easily be verified. Fourth and finally, our data set covers a period of more than 18 years and, hence, provides evidence invariant to business cycle considerations.

Although the use of survey data is widespread in order to proxy expected inflation rates as stated in equation (5.3), to date the academic literature that uses expectations of professional forecaster has so far mainly focused on whether or not central banks adopt Taylor-type rules. Reade (2006), for instance, uses monthly data of the University of Michigan survey to estimate Taylor rules for the Fed in a cointegrated VAR model. Using real-time data he provides support for the Taylor rule literature. Romer and Romer (2002) use the Livingston survey to compare inflation expectations with a simple forward-looking monetary-policy rule. Their results suggest that the monetary policy of the Fed differs between the sample periods. However, Reade (2006) and Romer and Romer (2002) only use the mean of the poll, whereas the CEF poll which is used in this chapter contains

[4]Mitchell and Pearce (2007), for instance, analyze the accuracy of the WSJ forecasts. They find that a majority of the professional forecasters produced unbiased interest rate forecasts, but the forecasts are indistinguishable from a random walk model and the economists are systematically heterogeneously distributed. Using a multivariate approach Eisenbeis, Waggoner and Zha (2002) evaluate the performance of professional forecasters in the WSJ poll relative to the other participants. Their results suggest that the dispersion in the forecasts may serve as an indication of how much uncertainty there may be about where the economy is going. Greer (2003) concentrates on the one-year forecast of the 30 year U.S. Treasury bond. He examines whether economists are able to predict the direction of change correctly and finds some evidence that it is indeed the case.

[5]In contrast to the view of Keane and Runkle (1990), Laster, Bennett and Geoum (1999) develop a model in which forecasters are rewarded for forecast accuracy in statistical terms as well as by publicity in case of giving the best forecast at a single point in time. As a consequence those forecasters will differ the most from consensus forecast whose wages depend the most on publicity.

individual data of over 300 business experts, which allows us to analyze the time as well as cross section dimension.[6]

Our study investigates whether professional forecasters believe in Taylor-type rules. Therefore, we use the monthly CEF poll for the time period between October 1989 and December 2007 covering 220 periods. The number of professional economists participating in the survey is the highest for the UK (75 forecaster) and the lowest for Canada (39 forecaster). Hence, our data set is an unbalanced panel. In order to investigate the time series characteristics of the expectation formation process of the participants, we only include professional forecasters who participated in the survey at least ten times during the period October 1989 - December 2007. This applies, for instance for the UK, to a total of 66 participants and yields over 5,000 forecasts for each variable, i.e. the expected three month interest rate, the expected Consumer Price Index (CPI) and the expected growth rate of the real Gross Domestic Product (GDP). Moreover, the professional forecasters are requested to predict the interest rates for two different time horizons, namely for the next three months and the following twelve months. Using these alternative time horizons we distinguish between a short-term and medium-term Taylor rule. Forecasts of the GDP and CPI are provided for the current and next year. In order to keep the forecast horizon constant (i.e. three and twelve months) we construct a weighted average of the GDP and CPI forecast as described in Appendix C.

Table 5.1 provides an overview of the data set and summarizes its main features. Table 5.1 also shows that the expectations on the macroeconomic variables were on average a good predictor for the future actual value. For instance, for Germany the average forecasts for the interest rate (4.61 percent) and inflation rate (2.13 percent) are close to the actual average values of 4.68 and 2.16 percent, respectively. Only for the UK the CPI forecasts (3.12 percent) differ noticeably from the actual value (3.38 percent). However, we leave the discussion of the accuracy of the forecasts to further research.

A potential drawback of our analysis is that the Taylor rule is suggested to work for the prime rate. Since our data set consists of three months interest rate forecasts this might contradict our analysis. However, Table 5.2 shows that the correlation coefficients between the actual three months interest

[6]Giordani and Soederlind (2001) point out that individual survey data on expectation are preferable to time series models, especially when forecast uncertainty is high. Using quarterly data, they analyze the uncertainty of U.S. inflation and real output growth forecasts of the Survey of Professional Forecasters and find that forecaster seem to underestimate uncertainty.

Table 5.1: Overview of the monthly data for the G7 countries

Country	Canada	France	Germany	Italy	Japan	UK	U.S.
Interest Rates Forecasts							
Short-term	5.12	4.91	4.61	6.45	1.70	6.65	4.37
Medium-term	5.27	4.77	4.63	6.27	1.79	6.58	4.70
Actual 3-months Interest Rate (mean)	5.27	5.13	4.68	6.61	1.72	6.69	4.68
Source OECD (1989 - 2007)							
CPI Forecasts							
Short-term	2.33	1.92	2.13	3.32	0.55	3.12	2.90
Medium-term	2.34	1.95	2.13	3.03	0.63	3.08	2.87
Actual CPI Growth (mean)	2.22	1.85	2.16	3.35	0.55	3.38	2.91
Source IMF (1989 - 2007)							
Real GDP Growth Forecast							
Short-term	2.59	2.02	1.68	1.62	1.63	2.01	2.76
Medium-term	2.73	2.18	1.82	1.82	1.68	2.17	2.74

Table 5.2: Correlation coefficients for the three months interest rate and the Funds rate

Central Bank (1989 - 2007)	Horizon	Mean (percent p.a.)	Correlation Coefficient
Federal Reserve	3 months	4.59	.99
	prime rate	4.43	(126.7)
Reserve Bank of Canada	3 months	5.31	.99
	prime rate	5.39	(180.8)
Bank of Japan	3 months	1.72	.99
	prime rate	1.35	(144.8)
Deutsche Bundesbank	3 months	4.69	.95
	prime rate	4.26	(45.8)
Bank of England	3 months	6.70	.99
	prime rate	6.55	(123.3)
Bank of France	3 months	5.14	.99
	prime rate	4.98	(128.1)
Bank of Italy	3 months	6.60	.99
	prime rate	6.53	(386.3)

Notes: Table 5.2 shows the mean of the three months and funds rate for the respective central bank; the Bravais-Pearson correlation coefficient measures the correlation of the three months interest rate and the prime rate over the sample period October 1989 - December 2007; t-value in parentheses test of significance of the correlation coefficients.

rate and the prime rate for the G7 countries are about 0.99. In addition, the application of the three months interest rate allows us to use data for France, Germany and Italy even after the introduction of the euro. Although the prime rate is the same among these three countries the three month interest rates differ among France, Germany and Italy. Therefore we decide to include the three countries even though the interest rate is mostly determined by the European Central Bank after 1999.

5.4 Estimation results

For our empirical analysis we start from the econometric specification of the Taylor rule as derived in section 5.2:

$$i_t = (1-\rho)(\bar{i} + \alpha_1 E_t(\pi_{t+k} - \pi^*) + \alpha_2 E_t(y_{t+q} - y^*_{t+q})) + \rho i_{t-1} + \nu_t (5.3)$$

In order to arrive at a testable relationship, the unobservable terms in equation (5.3) have to be eliminated. Since the data set we are using allows us to directly observe expectations on the short-term interest rate, the inflation rate and output changes, we only lack information on the equilibrium interest rate and the inflation target of the respective central bank. For the time being we treat them as time-invariant and aggregate both in the constant. Thus, we rewrite equation (5.3) as:

$$(5.4) \qquad E_t i_{t+l} = (1-\rho)\alpha_0 + \alpha_1(1-\rho)E_t\pi_{t+k} + \alpha_2(1-\rho)E_t(y_{t+q} - y^*_{t+q})$$

$$+\rho i_t + \epsilon_t$$

where $\alpha_0 = \bar{i} - \alpha_1 E_t \pi^*$

Due to data availability we have to use forecasts for output growth rather than for the output gap. For that reason we partly depart from specification (5.4) and estimate:

$$(5.5) \qquad E_t i_{t+1} = (1-\rho)\alpha_0 + \alpha_1(1-\rho)E_t\pi_{t+k} + \alpha_2(1-\rho)E_t(\Delta y_{t+q})$$

$$+\rho i_t + \epsilon_t$$

where the output gap has been substituted by the expected growth rate of output. More precisely, it is often argued in the literature that the central bank reacts to a deviation of the actual and/or expected growth rate of output from a target growth rate (i.e. an output growth gap). For convenience and in line with the literature we assume a constant target growth rate, which leads then to specification (5.5).

In equation (5.5) we already use the expected interest rate forecast as left-hand side variable. In the subsequent regressions we look at two different forecast horizons. We employ three months forecasts of the three months interest rate as the left-hand side variable when referring to the short-term forecast. For the medium-term forecast we employ the twelve months forecasts of the three months interest rate as the dependent variable. Note that we do not need to depart to the General Methods of Moments when estimating equation (5.5) since all expectational variables on the right-hand side are also observed data. Thus, we rely on OLS in our panel setting. However, our econometric analysis is impaired by the problem of overlapping forecast horizons since the monthly data set provides three months forecasts. This obviously leads to serial correlation in the error terms by construction. In order to overcome the problem of serial correlation in the error terms due to overlapping forecast horizons we apply a serial correlation model:

$$\epsilon_{t,i} = \beta_i \epsilon_{t-1,i} \tag{5.6}$$

where the autoregressive term β_i measures the degree of persistence in the error term. Additionally, we use Prais-Winsten panel corrected standard errors to account for cross section correlation among the survey participants.

Table 5.3 displays the results of estimating equation (5.5). The short-term and medium-term regressions are contemporaneous versions, i.e. all variables enter with the same time index. The short-term equation regresses the three months interest rate forecast on the forecasts of inflation and output growth for three months (i.e., $l = k = q = 3$). The medium-term regression uses forecast horizons of twelve months forecasts for all variables instead (i.e., $l = k = q = 12$). The lagged interest rate is the actual (observable) three months interest rate[7] and the timing is again as in the corresponding regressions before. In the forward-looking specification the dependent variable is the three months interest rate forecasts (i.e., $l = k = q = 3$) while the independent variables reflect twelve months forecasts (i.e., $l = k = q = 12$). Evaluating the estimations in Table 5.3 five findings stand out:

- First, for the short-term and the forward-looking version the interest rate forecasts are highly dominated by the actual rate which is indicated by a large smoothing parameter (ρ) between 0.66 (Italy, forward-looking version) and 0.95 (Japan, short-term version). Although the smoothing parameter estimated in our model is statistically smaller

[7] As actual interest rate we use the monthly average of the time series in order to avoid daily volatility effects. However, our results do not change applying the actual interest rate at the beginning or the end of the month. Results can be obtained on author's request.

than unity, it is very close to unity for some countries.[8] However, the high value of the smoothing parameter has also been documented in the literature that analyzes the actual central bank behavior. Using the same model set up but applying actual instead of expected values on the right hand side of equation (5.5), in principle, Clarida et al. (1998) estimate the G7 central banks' reaction function for the period between 1979 and 1993 and report similar smoothing parameters (Table 5.4). For instance, while we find smoothing parameters of 0.91, 0.95 and 0.92 for Germany, Japan, and the UK (short-term), Clarida et al. (1998) find values for these countries of about 0.91, 0.93 and 0.92, respectively. The medium-term forecasts, however, exhibit a smaller degree of smoothing of about 0.67, which is quite intuitive given the longer forecast horizon of twelve months and the likely perception that smoothing refers to avoiding pronounced short-term fluctuations. Hence, interest rate forecasts for the three-month horizon should exhibit a higher persistence compared to twelve months forecasts.

- Second, in the short-term and forward-looking version, the inflation coefficient (α_1) which is based on expectations is of reasonable size and in line with the Taylor rule in the case of Canada, France, Germany Italy, and the UK. For the US the inflation coefficient is not statistically different from unity. For Japan, the Taylor principle can be rejected on a one percent significance level.

- Third, in the medium-term version the inflation coefficient (α_1) is positive but significantly smaller than unity for all countries except for Italy. Put differently, financial market participants do not apply the Taylor principle by forecasting one year ahead interest rates for the majority of the G7 countries. Only, in the case of Italy the medium-term version displays a relationship in line with the Taylor principle.

- Fourth, in all specifications the output coefficient (α_2) has the expected sign for the G7 countries and is of reasonable magnitude. The expected output coefficient is highest for the UK (1.81, forward-looking version) and lowest for Italy (0.29, in the forward-looking version). The average of the output coefficients for all three versions is lower for Italy,

[8] This finding matches the well-demonstrated phenomenon that short-term expectations in financial markets are rather static than dynamic (Mitchell and Pearce, 2007). Furthermore, Krueger and Kuttner (1996) found that the Federal Funds future market provide efficient predictions on the future path of the prime rate. As the future and actual path of the prime rate are close to each other, static expectations seem reasonable as a means to forecast interest rates.

Japan and the U.S. implying that the financial markets believes that the monetary policy of these countries does not respond to expected output changes substantially. Interestingly, Clarida et al. (1998), in their analysis if the actual central bank behavior, report the lowest output coefficient for Japan and the U.S.. Apparently, the financial market integrates an understanding of differences in actual central bank reactions in forecasts of short-term interest rates.

- Fifth, the results reported in Table 5.3 basically support our choice of model specification. The coefficient of the autoregressive error term ranges between 0.53 (UK) and 0.89 (France). Hence, the application of a serial correlation model seems to be appropriate. Moreover, the overall coefficients of determination suggest a high explanatory power of the regression model.

Table 5.3 also shows an unreasonable size of the inflation coefficients for Japan (e.g. $\alpha_1 = 0.38$ in the short-term version). This is probably due to the severe monetary crisis in Japan during the 1990, when the monetary policy of the Bank of Japan was regarded as being ineffective (Westermann and Hutchinson, 2006). This view is also mirrored in the eyes of the financial market as the inflation coefficient for Japan is significantly smaller than unity and smallest among the G7 countries. In the short-term version the coefficient is only slightly different from zero. This implies that during the sample period the financial market's participants do not expect the Bank of Japan to substantial respond to inflation changes. However, one might also interpret this result as evidence that during the sample period the Bank of Japan had no inflation but a deflation problem and, therefore, did not considerably respond to inflationary pressure. In order to avoid the problems due to the monetary crisis in Japan we estimate the expected Taylor rule for the time period before and after the monetary instability. Table 5.5 shows the results excluding the period 1991 till 2003.[9] The results are now comparable to those for the other G7 central banks reported in Table 5.3. The Taylor principle holds for Japan at least in the forward-looking version and cannot be rejected in the short-and medium-term version. Interestingly, the output coefficient is only in line with the Taylor rule in the medium-term version, while it is ambiguous in the short-term and forward-looking version.

In sum, this section provides evidence that the financial market participant forecasts real and financial economic variables in a consistent way

[9] We choose to skip the years 1991 till 2003. However, the results are robust against other windows and available upon author's request.

Table 5.3: Taylor rule application with interest rate smoothing (October 1989 - December 2007)

Country		α_0	α_1	α_2	ρ	AR	R^2	Obs.	Groups
	Short	-.12*	1.23*	.84*	.86*	.64*	.97	3,213	33
		(.02)	(.10)	(.10)	(.01)				
Canada	Medium	.88*	.85*	.50*	.56*	.83*	.89	3,223	33
		(.12)	(.05)	(.06)	(.01)				
	Forward	-.19*	1.44*	.78*	.84*	.64*	.97	3,200	33
		(.03)	(.09)	(.11)	(.01)				
	Short	-.12*	1.63*	.66*	.74*	.71*	.96	3,518	33
		(.02)	(.09)	(.06)	(.01)				
France	Medium	.81*	.79*	.69*	.37*	.89*	.91	3,518	33
		(.01)	(.05)	(.04)	(.01)				
	Forward	-.38*	1.08*	.93*	.75*	.69*	.96	3,326	33
		(.02)	(.10)	(.07)	(.01)				
	Short	-.04*	1.08	1.13*	.91*	.60*	.99	5,156	44
		(.01)	(.10)	(.07)	(.01)				
Germany	Medium	.48*	.75*	.87*	.65*	.82*	.88	5,034	44
		(.01)	(.05)	(.04)	(.02)				
	Forward	-.15*	1.51*	1.14*	.89*	.60*	.99	5,122	44
		(.02)	(.07)	(.06)	(.01)				
	Short	-.50*	2.11*	.38*	.69*	.58*	.95	2,288	33
		(.03)	(.05)	(.07)	(.01)				
Italy	Medium	-.08*	1.65*	.45*	.46*	.76*	.94	2,258	33
		(.02)	(.05)	(.07)	(.01)				
	Forward	-.59*	2.25*	.29*	.66*	.61*	.96	2,268	33
		(.03)	(.04)	(.08)	(.01)				
	Short	.02*	.38+	.55*	.95*	.53*	.99	3,554	39
		(.00)	(.15)	(.08)	(.00)				
Japan	Medium	.21*	.81*	.53*	.80*	.74*	.98	2,884	39
		(.01)	(.08)	(.05)	(.01)				
	Forward	.00	.63*	.58*	.94*	.56*	.99	3,045	39
		(.01)	(.16)	(.11)	(.01)				
	Short	.02	1.44*	.85*	.92*	.55*	.98	5,484	66
		(.01)	(.07)	(.10)	(.01)				
UK	Medium	1.28*	.54*	.54*	.68*	.83*	.91	5,540	66
		(.01)	(.06)	(.05)	(.01)				
	Forward	-.15*	1.52*	1.81*	.94*	.54*	.99	5,630	66
		(.02)	(.12)	(.27)	(.01)				
	Short	-.24*	.93*	.50*	.85*	.69*	.97	2,833	40
		(.05)	(.09)	(.07)	(.01)				
USA	Medium	.16*	.76*	.72*	.69*	.80*	.89	2,712	39
		(.02)	(.08)	(.07)	(.01)				
	Forward	-.38*	1.03*	.68*	.85*	.69*	.97	2,743	39
		(.02)	(.10)	(.09)	(.01)				

Notes: Estimated equation (5.5) $E_t i_{t+1} = (1-\rho)\alpha_0 + \alpha_1(1-\rho)E_t\pi_{t+k} + \alpha_2(1-\rho)E_t(\Delta y_{t+q}) + \rho i_t + \epsilon_t$ by the means of a serial correlation model where $\epsilon_{t,i} = \beta_i \epsilon_{t-1,i}$; values in parentheses present panel corrected standard errors applying the Prais-Winsten model; the Hausman test reflects the level of significance that the random effects estimator is appropriate, otherwise the fixed effects estimator is used; R^2 refers to the overall fit; * (+) indicates significance at the one (ten) percent level, respectively.

Table 5.4: Estimation for Taylor rule with output gap and interest rate smoothing (Clardia Gali Gertler, NBER 6254)

Authors	Central Bank (Period)	Constant	GDP	CPI	Smoothing
CGG (1997)	Federal Reserve	0.26	.07*	1.79*	.92*
	(1979 to 1993)	(.85)	(.06)	(.18)	(.03)
CGG (1997)	Bank of Japan	1.21*	.08*	2.04*	.93*
	(1979 to 1993)	(.44)	(.03)	(.19)	(.01)
CGG (1997)	Deutsche Bundesbank	3.14*	.25*	1.31*	.91*
	(1979 to 1993)	(.28)	(.04)	(.09)	(.01)
CGG (1997)	Bank of England	5.76*	.19*	.98*	.92*
	(1979 to 1993)	(.69)	(.04)	(.09)	(.01)
CGG (1997)	Bank of France	5.75*	.88*	1.13*	.95*
	(1979 to 1993)	(.28)	(.10)	(.07)	(.01)
CGG (1997)	Bank of Italy	7.14*	.22*	.90*	.95*
	(1979 to 1993)	(.28)	(.08)	(.04)	(.01)

Notes: Table 5.4 shows the summary results of Tables 1 to 6 of Clarida, Gali and Gertler's (1997) article "Monetary Policy Rules in Practice: Some International Evidence"; * indicates significance at the one percent level.

Table 5.5: Taylor rule application for Japan with interest rate smoothing

Country	Japan		
Time Period	October 1989 - December 1990 and January 2004 - December 2007		
Horizon	Short	Medium	Forward
$(1-\rho)\alpha_0$	.06*	.16*	.10*
	(.01)	(.02)	(.01)
$(1-\rho)\alpha_1$	.06+	.18*	.11*
	(.03)	(.04)	(.03)
$(1-\rho)\alpha_2$	.00	.04+	-0.02
	(.01)	(.02)	(.01)
ρ	.96*	.83*	.95*
	(.01)	(.02)	(.01)
AR	.56*	.65*	.59*
α_1	1.59*	1.07*	2.31*
Chi^2-Test	(.41)	(.19)	(.37)
$\alpha_1 = 1$	.15	.72	.00
α_2	.07	.24+	-.43
Chi^2-Test	(.24)	(.12)	(.33)
$\alpha_2 = 0$	.76	.05	.19
R^2 within	.98	.91	.97
R^2 between	.99	.99	.99
R^2 overall	.99	.99	.99
Hausman	.00	.00	.00
Groups	955	833	877
Obs.	33	33	33

Notes: Estimated equation (5.5) $E_t i_{t+1} = (1-\rho)\alpha_0 + \alpha_1(1-\rho)E_t\pi_{t+k} + \alpha_2(1-\rho)E_t(\Delta y_{t+q}) + \rho i_t + \epsilon_t$ by the means of a serial correlation model where $\epsilon_{t,i} = \beta_i \epsilon_{t-1,i}$; values in parentheses present panel corrected standard errors applying the Prais-Winsten model; the Hausman test reflects the level of significance that the random effects estimator is appropriate, otherwise the fixed effects estimator is used; the Chi^2 tests whether the Taylor principle holds (i.e. $\alpha_1 > 1$); * (+) indicates significance at the one (ten) percent level, respectively.

with the Taylor rule in the short-term and forward-looking version. Especially, the latter version seems to be in line with market expectations. In the medium-term version expectations on six of the G7 central banks are not in line with the Taylor principle, i.e. the inflation coefficient is significantly smaller than unity. Additionally, we find that the output coefficient and the smoothing parameter have the expected sign and are of reasonable magnitude compared to the results reported by Clarida et al. (1998). Since we find evidence that the Taylor rule literature is very well reflected in financial market forecasts we now turn our analysis to the time period before the Taylor rule was established in the literature. Thus, section 5.5 focuses on the time period before the Taylor rule discussion started and analyzes whether financial market participants already adopted the Taylor rule, when the academia had not yet established Taylor-type rules.

5.5 Expectations on the Taylor rule prior to the Taylor rule literature

Although there exists a substantial body of Taylor rule papers in the literature the most influential articles are probably those of Taylor (1993) and Clarida et al. (1998) In the following analysis we therefore aim at examining the impact of these two papers on the expectation formation process of the financial market. In order to analyze whether the financial market was affected by the analysis of Clarida et al. (1998) we estimate the Taylor rule specification that has been established to be dominant in our previous analysis, namely the one including interest rate smoothing, for the time period October 1989 to November 1997.[10]

The results of the regression of equation (5.5) for this time period are presented in Table 5.6. Four finding stand out:

- First, in the short-term version the Taylor principle (i.e. $\alpha_1 > 1$) holds for Canada, France, Italy, and the UK. While for Germany and the U.S. the Taylor principle cannot be rejected as indicated by the Chi^2 test, we observe unreasonable small inflation coefficient violating the Taylor principle for Japan. The latter effect is probably due to the monetary situation in Japan discussed before.

[10]Clarida et al. (1998) published the first draft of the paper in November 1997 as a NBER working paper. Therefore, we exclude all periods after this date from the following analysis.

- Second, in the medium-term version the inflation coefficient (α_1) is significantly smaller than unity except for Italy. This again undermines our results obtained for the full sample period. In the forward-looking version the Taylor principle holds for 5 of the G7 countries while for the U.S. the Taylor principle cannot be rejected.

- Third, except for Italy (short-term and forward-looking versions) the output coefficients exhibit the expected positive sign and are statistically different from zero for all countries.

- Fourth, the smoothing parameters are again significant and of reasonable size compared to the values obtained for the full sample period. Additionally, the persistence of the error terms indicated by the significant autoregressive parameters supports our approach to apply a serial correlation model. Moreover, the overall coefficient of determination indicates high explanatory power.

In sum, we find that, for the majority of the G7 countries, the Taylor rule is already displayed in financial market forecasts prior to the analysis of Clarida et al. (1998). Put differently, the financial market did adopt Taylor-type rules already before the academia had identified them. This result is, overall, not surprising as apparently the central bank behavior for the G7 countries can also be referred to as Taylor rule based. In order to predict the short-term interest rate accurately, the financial market basically followed the central bank behavior and adopted this pattern in the forecasts even though it did not know about any specific behind it.

In a final step we now analyze whether the financial market adopts the Taylor rule prior to Taylor's publication in December 1993. Therefore, we only use forecasts provided between 1989 and 1993 and again estimate equation (5.5) including the interest rate smoothing behavior. Results are presented in Table 5.7. The Taylor principle holds for Canada, France, Germany, Italy, the UK and in the forward-looking version for Japan. While we have to reject the Taylor principle for Japan (short- and medium-term version), we find ambiguous inflation coefficients for the U.S.. The output coefficients are significant for all countries examined and of comparable magnitude to our previous results. Except in case of Italy and the UK the output coefficients are not significantly positive. For Italy we find an insignificant output coefficient implying that the financial market does not expect the interest rate to change if output changes. For the UK we find significantly negative output coefficients. This result is probably driven by the monetary

Table 5.6: Taylor rule application with interest rate smoothing before CGG (1997)

Country		α_0	α_1	α_2	ρ	AR	R^2	Obs.	Groups
	Short	.09*	1.31*	.76*	.83*	.62*	.97	1,500	26
		(.05)	(.13)	(.14)	(.01)				
Canada	Medium	1.67*	.84*	.32*	.50*	.82*	.89	1,493	26
		(.04)	(.04)	(.07)	(.02)				
	Forward	.10+	1.43*	.55*	.80*	.62*	.97	1,492	26
		(.05)	(.13)	(.14)	(.02)				
	Short	-.59*	2.80*	.40*	.63*	.61*	.96	1,477	25
		(.04)	(.10)	(.06)	(.01)				
France	Medium	2.44*	.51*	.42*	.20*	.95*	.91	1,365	25
		(.01)	(.08)	(.05)	(.02)				
	Forward	-.66*	2.73*	.43*	.65*	.61*	.96	1,368	25
		(.04)	(.11)	(.08)	(.01)				
	Short	-.17*	.96*	2.19*		.48*	.99	2,105	31
		(.02)	(.44)	(.39)	(.01)				
Germany	Medium	.53*	.93*	.73*	.62*	.84*	.88	2,057	31
		(.01)	(.10)	(.06)	(.02)				
	Forward	-.40*	2.15*	1.71*	.92*	.48*	.99	2,061	31
		(.02)	(.17)	(.19)	(.01)				
	Short	.62*	1.83*	-.05	.53*	.54*	.95	890	17
		(.17)	(.07)	(.09)	(.02)				
Italy	Medium	.48*	1.71*	.20+	.39*	.69*	.94	856	17
		(.08)	(.07)	(.10)	(.02)				
	Forward	.33*	2.04*	-.12	.55*	.55*	.96	855	17
		(.08)	(.08)	(.11)	(.02)				
	Short	-.02	.21	1.09*	.93*	.50*	.99	1,739	30
		(.01)	(.20)	(.12)	(.01)				
Japan	Medium	.30*	.63*	.67*	.74*	.71*	.98	1,365	30
		(.02)	(.11)	(.08)	(.02)				
	Forward	-.08*	.64*	1.13*	.92*	.54*	.99	1,407	30
		(.01)	(.22)	(.16)	(.01)				
	Short	.11*	1.42*	.54*	.90*	.52*	.98	257	52
		(.03)	(.07)	(.12)	(.01)				
UK	Medium	1.91*	.54*	.20*	.65*	.80*	.91	2,986	52
		(.02)	(.05)	(.07)	(.02)				
	Forward	-.14*	1.62*	1.48*	.94*	.51*	.99	2,957	51
		(.03)	(.16)	(.41)	(.01)				
	Short	-.15*	.75*	.61*	.86*	.62*	.97	1,154	31
		(.09)	(.14)	(.11)	(.01)				
USA	Medium	.28*	.79*	.59*	.72*	.74*	.89	1,121	32
		(.18)	(.13)	(.12)	(.02)				
	Forward	-.38*	.86*	1.11*	.88*	.59*	.97	1,127	32
		(.10)	(.17)	(.20)	(.01)				

Notes: Estimated equation (5.5) $E_t i_{t+1} = (1-\rho)\alpha_0 + \alpha_1(1-\rho)E_t\pi_{t+k} + \alpha_2(1-\rho)E_t(\Delta y_{t+q}) + \rho i_t + \epsilon_t$ by the means of a serial correlation model where $\epsilon_{t,i} = \beta_i \epsilon_{t-1,i}$; values in parentheses present panel corrected standard errors applying the Prais-Winsten model; the Hausman test reflects the level of significance that the random effects estimator is appropriate, otherwise the fixed effects estimator is used; the Chi^2 tests whether the Taylor principle holds (i.e. $\alpha_1 > 1$); * (+) indicates significance at the one (ten) percent level, respectively.

Table 5.7: Taylor rule application with interest rate smoothing before Taylor (1993)

Country		α_0	α_1	α_2	ρ	AR	R^2	Obs.	Groups
Canada	Short	-.35*	1.87*	1.00*	.78*	.58*	.97	832	23
		(.07)	(.15)	(.16)	(.02)				
	Medium	1.54*	.99*	.33*	.47*	.80*	.89	827	23
		(.06)	(.09)	(.08)	(.03)				
	Forward	-.28	1.89*	.57*	.74*	.57*	.97	849	23
		(.20)	(.13)	(.15)	(.02)				
France	Short	.97*	1.93*	.67*	.46*	.45*	.96	657	21
		(.13)	(.15)	(.05)	(.02)				
	Medium	.57*	1.53*	1.00*	.31*	.74*	.91	593	21
		(.07)	(.12)	(.09)	(.03)				
	Forward	.33*	1.96*	1.01*	.53*	.50*	.96	595	21
		(.10)	(.15)	(.10)	(.02)				
Germany	Short	-.08	1.61*	1.19*	.89*	.36*	.99	1,049	24
		(.08)	(.31)	(.13)	(.02)				
	Medium	.02	1.13*	1.13*	.66*	.76*	.88	1,016	24
		(.06)	(.17)	(.10)	(.03)				
	Forward	-.33*	2.03*	1.62*	.91*	.34*	.99	1,018	24
		(.08)	(.33)	(.23)	(.02)				
Italy	Short	1.42*	1.51*	.27	.54*	.51*	.95	444	14
		(.23)	(.18)	(.17)	(.03)				
	Medium	1.43*	1.49*	.14	.41*	.64*	.94	437	14
		(.17)	(.13)	(.18)	(.03)				
	Forward	.94*	1.85*	-.20	.56*	.54*	.96	437	12
		(.20)	(.18)	(.22)	(.03)				
Japan	Short	-.03	-.07	1.41*	.92*	.48*	.99	921	23
		(.03)	(.38)	(.23)	(.02)				
	Medium	.43*	.77*	.60*	.69*	.66*	.98	769	23
		(.03)	(.14)	(.09)	(.03)				
	Forward	-.21*	1.88*	.57*	.94*	.51*	.99	814	23
		(.06)	(.49)	(.28)	(.02)				
UK	Short	-.07	1.53*	-.32	.93*	.41*	.98	1,534	44
		(.04)	(.13)	(.22)	(.01)				
	Medium	1.85*	.51*	-.38*	.67*	.71*	.91	1,565	44
		(.05)	(.07)	(.10)	(.02)				
	Forward	-.22*	1.99*	.60	.97*	.41*	.99	1,534	44
		(.05)	(.44)	(.66)	(.01)				
USA	Short	-.08	.80*	.33*	.82*	.60*	.97	533	27
		(.06)	(.18)	(.14)	(.02)				
	Medium	.71*	.66*	.29*	.68*	.73*	.89	506	27
		(.05)	(.14)	(.14)	(.04)				
	Forward	-.31*	.93*	.60*	.84*	.58	.97	509	27
		(.06)	(.20)	(.21)	(.02)				

Notes: Estimated equation (5.5) $E_t i_{t+1} = (1-\rho)\alpha_0 + \alpha_1(1-\rho)E_t\pi_{t+k} + \alpha_2(1-\rho)E_t(\Delta y_{t+q}) + \rho i_t + \epsilon_t$ by the means of a serial correlation model where $\epsilon_{t,i} = \beta_i \epsilon_{t-1,i}$; values in parentheses present panel corrected standard errors applying the Prais-Winsten model; the Hausman test reflects the level of significance that the random effects estimator is appropriate, otherwise the fixed effects estimator is used; * (+) indicates significance at the one (ten) percent level, respectively.

crisis that the UK experienced during the observation period of 1998 to 1993. Since the UK increased interest rates substantially in 1992 which caused the British pound to leave the ERM II and simultaneously the UK experienced low growth rates the output coefficient enters equation (5.5) with a negative sign. After the ERM II crisis the UK monetary policy shifted towards lower short-term interest rates, and an inflation target was announced (Söderlind, 2000).

An explanation of why the financial market adopted the Taylor rule prior to the original publication of Taylor might be that central banks themselves had applied them to set the short-term interest rate. This has been documented in the literature (Clarida et al. 1998).

5.6 Conclusion

This chapter investigates whether the academic research on the Taylor rule diffuses into financial market forecasts or whether the Taylor rule has already been adopted by the financial market prior to be recognized by the academia. Therefore, we use the CEF poll to analyze whether professional economic forecasters believe in and, thus, apply Taylor-type rules for their forecasts for the G7 countries. Three findings stand out: First, we find that interest rate forecasts are, indeed, internally consistent with the message of Taylor-type rules for all G7 countries. In the case of Japan we obtain this result by neglecting the period of monetary instability. Second, we provide evidence that medium-term forecasts display the Taylor rule to a lesser extent, if at all. Third, applying the data set for the time period before the introduction of the Taylor rule in 1993 clearly shows that the financial market already adopted the Taylor rule, when the academia was not yet aware of this type of monetary rule.

In sum, chapter 5 provides strong evidence that the financial markets adopts Taylor-type rules to forecasts short-term interest rates for the G7 countries. The subsequent chapter 6 investigates whether this feature is inherent in financial market forecasts for emerging markets and questions whether the adoption of an inflation targeting regime has an impact in the expectations formation process.

Chapter 6

Does Inflation Targeting matter? - Evidence from the expectation formation process in emerging markets

6.1 Introduction

In the 1980s Latin-American countries experienced the highest inflation rates of above 200 percent per year in the world. In contrast, in 2006 they managed to have on average an inflation rate of about 6 percent. A similar process was observed for the central and eastern European countries during the 1990s. They reduced their inflation rates substantially from on average 45 percent p.a. in the 1990'ies down to on average 5 percent p.a. in 2007. This process of stabilizing prices has been achieved under different monetary and exchange rate regimes, ranging from the adoption of inflation targeting combined with floating exchange rates to the abandonment of independent monetary policy by introducing currency boards or even by dollarization of the economy.

Inflation targeting has been adopted, for instance, by Brazil, Chile, the Czech Republic, Hungary, Mexico, and Poland. This raises the question: Does inflation targeting matter for the performance of the economy? Many empirical studies have focused on this issue. However, most studies have so far concentrated on the impact of inflation targeting on variables that are directly observable like output, unemployment and inflation. While these studies clearly show that the adoption of inflation targeting has significantly reduced inflation, the literature has not yet found a consensus whether the reduction of inflation is accompanied by a change in output growth.[1]

The fact that most empirical studies focus on actual economic performance of inflation targeting countries means that there is a lack in empirical research, because it is often argued that - in the first place - inflation targeting has important consequences for the expectation formation process which, in turn, leads to different economic performances. This chapter contribute to close this gap in research by examining whether the introduction of inflation targeting has systematically changed expectation formation process in financial markets. Since there is a close theoretical link between inflation targeting and Taylor rules, the performance of a group of ten (inflation targeting and non-inflation targeting) emerging markets is evaluated by the means of the expected Taylor rules. More precisely, we investigate whether financial markets expect the central bank to behave in a manner in line with the well-known Taylor rule.

This chapter, thus, changes the perspective on interest rate rules from the typical use in the academic literature as a reaction function to explaining central bank behavior. We use data from the CEF poll and investigate whether Taylor rules are present in the expectation formation process for emerging market variables. The data set includes Argentina, Brazil, Chile, Czech Republic, Hungary, Mexico, Poland, Slovakia, Turkey, and Venezuela. Since this country group includes inflation targeting and non-inflation targeting countries, we are able to test whether the adoption of inflation targeting matters for expectation formation process.

In order to do so, this chapter is structured as follows: The subsequent section briefly reviews the theoretical link between inflation targeting

[1]While Mishkin and Schmidt-Hebbel (2006) find that inflation targeting helps countries to achieve lower inflation rates in the medium-term. Their evidence does not suggest that countries that adopt inflation targeting attain better monetary policy performance relative to non-inflation targeting countries. By analyzing 15 inflation targeting countries Landerrechte et al. (2001) find that output growth suffers in inflation targeting regimes. Whereas Brito and Bysted (2006) show that inflation targeting is an efficient monetary policy to decrease the level and volatility of inflation in 13 Latin-American countries, but that the adoption of inflation targeting is not accompanied by a change in output growth or higher volatility in interest rates. Corbo and Schmidt-Hebbel (2001) compare inflation targeting in five Latin-American countries to other inflation targeting countries. They conclude that the adoption of inflation targeting is correlated with a large decline in output volatility. Finally, Corbo et al. (2002) find that inflation targeting countries have succeeded in reducing output costs of stabilization and in strengthening policy credibility.

and interest rate rules as well as the empirical concept of Taylor-type rules. Section 6.3 explains the data set. Section 6.4 presents the empirical results for inflation targeting and non-inflation targeting countries. the group of inflation targetors is examined in more detail in section 6.5 in which we study the importance of the time-varying inflation target and the credibility issue. Finally, section 6.6 concludes.

6.2 The theoretical and empirical morphology of Taylor-type rules

All major central banks in industrial countries currently conduct monetary policy by using market-oriented instruments in order to influence the short-term interest rate. Since the seminal paper of Taylor (1993), it has virtually become a convention to describe the interest rate setting behavior of central banks in terms of monetary policy reaction functions. In its plain form, the so-called Taylor rule states that the short-term interest rate, i.e., the instrument of a central bank, reacts to deviations of inflation and output from their respective target levels. Although the Taylor rule started out as an empirical exercise, there is a clear theoretical link between inflation targeting and Taylor rules. Svensson (1997) showed that a Taylor rule can be derived as the explicit solution of an optimal control problem within a stylized macro model which we briefly review subsequently.

Aggregate demand is described by the conventional dynamic IS-relation of the following form:

$$\hat{y}_{t+1} = \beta_1 \hat{y}_t - \beta_2 (i_t - \pi_t) + \eta_{t+1} \tag{6.1}$$

where $\hat{y}$ is the output gap defined as the deviation of real GDP from its natural rate, i is the short-term nominal interest rate that is also the instrument of the central bank and $\pi = p_t - p_{t-1}$ is the annual inflation rate with p representing the aggregate price level. All variables except the interest rate are expressed in natural logarithms. The term η is an i.i.d. shock variable with zero mean representing demand shocks. The structural parameters are such that $\beta_2 > 0$ and $0 < \beta_1 < 1$.

Aggregate supply is expressed in terms of the Phillips curve relation:

$$\pi_{t+1} = \pi_t + \alpha_1 \hat{y}_t + \epsilon_{t+1} \tag{6.2}$$

where ϵ represents an i.i.d. random cost-push shock, and the parameter $\alpha_1 > 0$ determines the slope of the short-term Phillips curve. Equation (6.2) states that inflation changes according to the size of the output gap and the supply shocks.

The central bank aims at minimizing the following intertemporal loss function with the size of inflation and the output gap as the two arguments:

$$\min E_t = \sum_{\tau=t}^{\infty} \delta^{\tau-t} L(\pi_\tau, \hat{y}_\tau), \tag{6.3}$$

where $0 < \delta < 1$ represents the discount factor. The period loss function is specified as:

$$L(\pi_\tau, \hat{y}_\tau) = \frac{1}{2}[(\pi_\tau - \pi^*)^2 + \lambda \hat{y}_\tau^2] \tag{6.4}$$

where π^* is the inflation target defined by the monetary authority and λ is the relative weight that is attached to stabilize output. For $\lambda > 0$ such preferences are usually described as *variable inflation targeting*, whereas a zero weight on output expresses a strategy of *strict inflation targeting.*

Optimizing the intertemporal loss function under the constraints of the structure of the economy displayed by the IS- and the Phillips curve leads to an optimal behavior that is commonly characterized as *inflation-forecast targeting*:

$$\pi_{t+2|t} - \pi^* = -\frac{\lambda}{\delta \alpha_1 k} \hat{y}_{t+1|t}, \tag{6.5}$$

$$\textit{with} \;\; k = \frac{1}{2}\left(1 - \frac{\lambda(1-\delta)}{\delta \alpha_1^2} + \sqrt{1 + \frac{\lambda(1-\delta)}{\delta \alpha_1^2} + \frac{4\lambda}{\alpha_1^2}}\right) \geq 1,$$

where $x_{t+j|t}$ denotes the expectations in time t of a variable x for j periods ahead t.[2] The two-period-ahead inflation forecast, $\pi_{t+j|t}$, should equal the inflation target only if the one-period-ahead output forecast equals the natural output rate, that is, if the expected next period's output gap, $\hat{y}_{t+1|t}$, is zero. Otherwise it should exceed (fall short of) the inflation target in proportion to how much the one-period output forecast falls short of (exceeds) the natural level of output. The proportionality is increasing in the relative weight λ. This essentially displays the gradual inflation stabilization strategy

[2] That is, $E_t[x_{t+j}] \equiv x_{t+j|t}$.

under variable inflation targeting. A higher weight on output stabilization leads to a slower adjustment of the inflation rate.

Solving the demand and supply equations for the respective expectations and substituting them into the optimality condition (6.5) yields a specific reaction function of the Taylor rule form:

$$i_t = \pi_t + \tilde{b}_1(\pi_t - \pi^*) + \tilde{b}_2\hat{y}_t, \tag{6.6}$$

$$where\ \tilde{b}_1 = \frac{1-c}{\beta_2\alpha_1},\ \tilde{b}_2 = \frac{1-c+\beta_1}{\beta_2}\ and\ c = \frac{\lambda}{\lambda+\delta\alpha_1^2 k}$$

For the purpose of empirical exercises Clarida et al. (1998) proposed a forward-looking variant of the Taylor rule which takes into account the preemptive nature of monetary policy as well as interest smoothing behavior of central banks. This particular type of reaction function has become very popular in applied empirical research. Although it is still in the spirit of the Taylor rule, specifications of this type represent a modification of the original Taylor rule and, thus, the literature often refers to them as Taylor-type rules. Following Clarida et al. (1998, 2000) the baseline forward-looking policy rule takes the form:

$$i_t^* = \bar{i} + \alpha_1 E_t(\pi_{t+k} - \pi^*) + \alpha_2 E_t(y_{t+q} - y_{t+q}^*), \tag{6.7}$$

where i^* is the desired level of the nominal short-term interest rate, and $\bar{i}$ is its equilibrium level.[3] The second term on the right-hand side is the expected deviation of the k-period ahead inflation rate (π) from the target rate (π^*) which is assumed to be constant over time.[4] The third term is the expected deviation of the q-period ahead level of output (y) from its natural level (y^*) (i.e., the expected output gap $E[\hat{y}_t]$). The coefficients α_1 and α_2 which will be the center of our estimates represent the reaction coefficients.[5] The assumption of interest rate smoothing behavior implies that:

$$i_t = (1-\rho)i_t^* + \rho i_{t-1} + \nu_t, \tag{6.8}$$

[3]The difference in the first term on the right hand side of 6.6 and 6.7 arises from the fact that the model of Svensson (1997) normalizes the equilibrium real interest rate to zero.

[4]In the subsequent analysis we allow π^* to be time variant. This actually fits reality very well against the background that inflation targeting countries frequently announce inflation targets reflecting nothing else than the desired long-term inflation rate. As these countries are trying to decrease the perceived long-term inflation level they are announcing decreasing inflation targets.

[5]We changed the notation to indicate that in our empirical exercises we do not estimate the optimal rule that we derived before.

where the parameter ρ (with $0 < \rho < 1$) describes the degree of interest rate smoothing and ν_t represents an i.i.d. exogenous random shock to the interest rate. Combining 6.7 and 6.8 leads to

$$i_t = (1-\rho)(\bar{i} + \alpha_1 E_t(\pi_{t+k} - \pi^*) + \alpha_2 E_t(y_{t+q} - y^*_{t+q})) + \rho i_{t-1} + \nu_t \quad (6.9)$$

Equation (6.9) represents the econometric specification which is commonly used to describe central bank behavior.[6] It is reduced to the plain Taylor rule when ρ is assumed to be zero and the horizons of the forward-looking behavior of the central bank, k and q, are also set equal to zero in econometric exercises.

The main messages generated by empirical studies focusing on central bank behavior can be summarized as follows. First, forward-looking specifications seem to fit the central banks' behavior better than contemporaneous versions. Here the forward-looking feature is most relevant for the inflation gap with the horizon (k) being about one year. Second, the relevance of the Taylor principle for stability, which is a reaction coefficient for inflation being greater than unity, is well demonstrated and its presence is a strong feature for most central banks. Third, the reaction coefficient for the output gap is mostly significant but has a significant lower level compared to the inflation gap coefficient.[7] Fourth, persistence in the short-term interest rate is a strong feature in the data. However, what is not yet clear is whether this is due to intended interest rate smoothing or whether it is due to a strong autocorrelation in the shocks upon which monetary policy reacts.[8]

Our empirical analysis takes the afore-mentioned four empirical core results of Taylor-type rules as its starting point and interprets them as (historical) information that is available for financial market participants. We also assume that the agents in the financial market are aware of the theoretical link between inflation targeting and Taylor rules, that is that they in

---

[6]Since it contains expectations on the right-hand side that are not directly observable it is common to substitute them by the observed ex-post levels of the respective variables and rearrange the estimation equation into a form that contains the expectation errors of the central bank in the error term. This form is then estimated based on the General Methods of Moments.

[7]In particular, for the output gap the literature demonstrated that it is relevant to discriminate between ex post and real-time data (Orphanides, 2001). Since we use observed expected variables in our analysis we do not need to take effects arising from ex post data into consideration.

[8]Again, since this issue is also not of a strong concern in the present chapter, we refer to the recent literature. See, for instance, Rudebusch (2006).

particular expect inflation targeting countries to be well described by Taylor-type rules. If, in turn, the agents believe in the Taylor-type rules and take this kind of analysis seriously, we would expect to observe this in their joint forecasts for the short-term interest rate, the inflation rate and the output development. In this case, the joint forecasts of the three variables can hardly be independent from each other. They should rather display the same links and dependencies that the estimated reaction functions of the central banks tell us. In addition, because of the theoretical link between inflation targeting and Taylor rules, this form of expectation formation should be more relevant for inflation targeting countries compared to non-inflation targeting countries. We therefore estimate variants of equation (6.9) based on reported forecasts of financial market participants to answer the question that we raised in the title. Before we present the results, the next section briefly introduces our data set.

6.3 The data set

We use data from a survey conducted by the CEF. The survey regularly asks professional forecasters about their projection of several financial and real economy variables such as short-term interest rates, unemployment rates and real GDP forecasts. The survey includes data for several countries. Since our analysis requires forecasts for short-term interest rates, our data set is limited to ten emerging markets, namely Argentina, Brazil, Chile, the Czech Republic, Hungary, Mexico, Poland, Slovakia, Turkey, and Venezuela. Out of this group, seven economies adopted officially inflation targets: Brazil, Chile, the Czech Republic, Hungary, Mexico, Poland and Slovakia.[9] We refer to them as the inflation targeting countries as opposed to non-inflation targeting countries.

This data set has several advantages over other surveys and is, thus, less subject to some of the weaknesses often associated with survey data. First, the individual forecasts are published together with the name of the employer of the forecaster. Given that this allows everybody to evaluate the performance of the individual participants, the accuracy of the forecasts can

[9]Since Slovakia introduced the inflation targeting system as of 2007 we treat Slovakia as a non-inflation targeting country in our study. This can be justified since the time period being a non-inflation targeting country prevails the sample period.

be expected to have an effect on the reputation of the forecasters.[10] This is expected to increase the incentives of the survey participants to submit their very best rather than strategic forecasts (see Keane and Runkle, 1990).[11] Second, unlike some other surveys, forecasters participating in the CEF poll do not only submit the direction of the expected change of the macroeconomic variable, but forecast a specific level. Third, the survey data are readily available to the public so that our results can easily be verified.

For the five Latin-American countries in our sample the survey provides monthly data for the period from April 2001 to December 2007, hence our analysis covers 81 periods. During this time period 245 institutions participated at least in one survey. For the central and eastern European countries the survey is conducted on a bimonthly basis for the period from May 1998 to December 2007. It includes forecasts of 163 institutions over 63 periods. In order to investigate the time series characteristics of the expectation formation process, we only include professional forecasters participating in at least ten polls.[12] This applies to a total of 128 (116) participants and yields 5,433 (3,722) forecasts for the Latin-American (central and eastern European) countries.

The professional forecasters are requested to predict the economic variables for two different time horizons. The survey provides CPI and real GDP forecasts for the current and next year while the short-term interest is requested to be predicted for the next three and twelve months. Hence, this information covers forecast periods of three and twelve months. In order to equalize the beginning and end of the forecast period, we generate a

[10]Mitchell and Pearce (2007a), for instance, analyze the accuracy of the Wall Street Journal (WSJ) forecasts. They find that a majority of the professional forecasters produced unbiased interest rate forecasts, but the forecasts are indistinguishable from a random walk model and the economists are systematically heterogeneously distributed. Using a multivariate approach Eisenbeis, Waggoner and Zha (2002) evaluate the performance of professional forecasters in the WSJ poll relative to the other participants. Their results suggest that the dispersion in the forecasts may serve as an indication of how much uncertainty there may be about where the economy is going. Greer (2003) concentrates on the one-year forecast of the 30 year U.S. Treasury bond. He examines whether economists are able to predict the direction of change correctly and finds some evidence that it is indeed the case.

[11]In contrast to the view of Keane and Runkle (1990), Laster, Bennett and Geoum (1999) develop a model in which forecasters are rewarded for forecast accuracy in statistical terms as well as by publicity in case of giving the best forecast at a single point in time. As a consequence those forecasters will differ the most from the consensus forecast whose wages depend the most on publicity.

[12]We also used other minimum participation rates. The results, however, do not change and are available upon request.

synthetic short-term and medium-term CPI and GDP forecast by weighting the forecast with the remaining months at the time of the forecast. This procedure is quite common in the literature (Heppke-Falk and Hüffner, 2004, and Beck, 2001). For instance, the synthetic medium-term forecast in July is the weighted average of the GDP of the current and next year while the synthetic short-term forecast is, of course, the forecast of the current year only. Appendix C provides an overview of the calculation of the synthetic short-term and medium-term forecasts. Using these alternative time horizons we distinguish between a short-term and a medium-term Taylor rule specification.

Table 6.1 and 6.2 summarize the main features of the data set. The predicted interest rate is either the Funds rate or a three-month interest rate. Since the Taylor rule is suggested to work for the Funds rate our data set seems to have a deficiency in case of Hungary, Poland, Slovakia and the Czech Republic as the forecasted series is a three-month interest rate only. However, the correlation coefficient between the actual three-month rate and the Funds rate for these countries is about 0.98. Hence, this should not diminish the quality of our empirical analysis. Tables 6.1 and 6.2 also show that the expectations on the macroeconomic variables are on average a good predictor of their actual value. For instance, the forecasts for the Mexican interest rate (7.8 percent) and inflation rate (4.3 percent) are close to the actual values of 7.7 and 4.4 percent, respectively. Only for Venezuela the forecasts differ from the actual values. While the financial market overestimated both the inflation and the interest rate by about 5 percent, their real interest rate forecasts were correct. However, we leave the discussion of the accuracy of the forecasts to further research and turn to the empirical analysis of the expectation formation process in emerging markets.

6.4 Estimation results

For our empirical analysis we start from the econometric specification of the Taylor-type rule as derived in section 6.2:

$$i_t = (1-\rho)(\bar{i} + \alpha_1 E_t(\pi_{t+k} - \pi^*) + \alpha_2 E_t(y_{t+q} - y^*_{t+q})) + \rho i_{t-1} + \nu_t \quad (6.9)$$

In order to arrive at a testable relationship, the unobservable terms in equation (6.9) have to be eliminated. Next we modify equation (6.9) in the way that we use the expected interest rate $E_t i_{t+1}$ as the dependent variable rather

Table 6.1: Overview of the monthly data for the Latin-American countries (2001 - 2007)

Country Introduction of Inflation Targeting	Argentina No	Brazil since June 1999	Mexico since January 1999	Venezuela No	Chile since January 1991
Interest Rate	BAIBOR	Funds Rate	Funds Rate	Funds Rate	MPR
Forecasts					
Short-term	12.8	17.7	7.8	16.1	3.8
Medium-term	12.2	15.6	7.7	16.0	4.4
Interest Rate Series	BAIBOR	Funds Rate	Funds Rate	Interbank Rate	MPR
Mean	13.0	18.1	7.7	11.1	3.7
Source	BCRA	OECD	BDM	BCV	BCC
GDP Growth					
Forecasts					
Short-term	3.2	2.8	2.9	2.0	4.4
Medium-term	3.5	3.0	3.2	2.7	4.5
CPI Forecasts	CPI	IPCA	CPI	CPI	CPI
Short-term	16.4	6.5	4.3	23.7	2.9
Medium-term	12.1	6.1	4.2	23.2	2.9
CPI series	CPI	IPCA	CPI	CPI	CPI
Mean	17.8	7.8	4.4	18.5	2.7
Real Interest Rate					
Forecasts					
Short-term	-3.6	10.8	3.6	-7.9	0.9
Medium-term	-2.4	9.2	3.6	-7.8	1.6

than the actual interest rate. Since we are able to directly observe the expectations on the short-term interest rate, the inflation rate and the output development, we only lack information on the equilibrium interest rate and the inflation target of the respective central bank. Given the short sample period we treat them as time-invariant for the time being and summarize both in the constant.[13] Thus, we rewrite equation (6.9) as:

$$E_t i_{t+1} = (1-\rho)\alpha_0 + \alpha_1(1-\rho)E_t\pi_{t+k} + \alpha_2(1-\rho)E_t(y_{t+q} - y^*_{t+q}) \tag{6.10}$$

$$+\rho i_t + \epsilon_t$$

$$where \alpha_0 = \bar{i} - \alpha_1 E_t \pi^* \tag{6.11}$$

Due to data availability we have to use forecasts for output growth

[13] In the subsequent section 6.5 we allow for an observable time varying inflation target, when we limit our analysis to the inflation targeting countries only. At this point of the analysis we do not account for the inflation target because it is not observable for the non-inflation targeting countries and we want to treat both groups identically in our regression specification.

Table 6.2: Overview of the monthly data for the central and eastern European countries (1998 – 2007)

Country Introduction of Inflation Targeting	Czech Rep. since January 1999	Hungary since December 2001	Poland since January 1990	Slovakia since January 2007	Turkey No
Interest Rate Forecasts	3 months PRIBOR	Treasury bill Rate	Interbank Rate	3 months BRIBOR	Interbank Rate
Short-term	4.3	9.6	9.4	7.5	35.4
Medium-term	4.6	8.6	8.7	7.0	28.5
Actual 3-months Interest Rate	3-months PRIBOR	90-Day Treasury bill Rate	3-month Interbank Rate	3 months BRIBOR Rate	Overnight Interbank
Mean	4.4	10.3	9.9	7.7	39.3
Source	OECD	OECD	OECD	OECD	OECD
GDP Growth Forecasts					
Short-term	3.2	3.7	4.3	4.6	3.6
Medium-term	3.4	3.8	4.4	4.6	3.8
CPI Forecasts	CPI	CPI	CPI	CPI	CPI
Short-term	3.4	7.1	4.4	6.4	33.2
Medium-term	3.7	5.6	4.2	5.3	23.9
CPI series	CPI	CPI	CPI	CPI	CPI
Mean	3.2	7.0	3.9	6.1	31.2
Real Interest Rate Forecasts					
Short-term	0.9	2.6	5.0	1.2	3.0
Medium-term	1.1	2.2	4.3	1.1	-0.6

rather than for the output gap (or level respectively). For that reason we modify specification (6.10) to

$$E_t i_{t+1} = (1-\rho)\alpha_0 + \alpha_1(1-\rho)E_t\pi_{t+k} + \alpha_2(1-\rho)E_t(\Delta y_{t+q}) + \rho i_t + \epsilon_t \tag{6.12}$$

where the output gap has been substituted by the growth rate of output (Δy_{t+q}).[14]

In equation (6.12) we already use the expected short-term interest rate forecast as the left-hand side variable. In the subsequent regressions we

[14]This substitution can be justified as follows: it is often argued in the literature that the central bank reacts to a deviation of the actual respectively expected growth rate of output from a target growth rate (i.e. an output growth gap). Since our sample period is quite small we assume a constant target growth rate, which leads then to specification (6.12). However, we are aware that the output gap coefficient, thus, does not have the same structural interpretation we have given before.

look at two different forecast horizons. We apply three month forecasts of the short-term interest rate as the left-hand side variable when referring to the short-term forecast. For the medium-term forecast we use the twelve months forecasts of the short-term interest rate as the dependent variable. Note that we do not need to apply the General Methods of Moments when estimating equation (6.12), since all expectational variables on the right-hand side are also observed data. Thus, we rely on OLS in our panel setting. However, our econometric analysis is impaired by the problem of overlapping forecast horizons since the monthly data set provides three months forecasts. This obviously leads to serial correlation in the error terms by construction. In order to overcome this problem we apply a serial correlation model:

$$\epsilon_{t,i} = \beta_{t,1}\epsilon_{t-1,i} \tag{6.13}$$

where the autoregressive term β measures the degree of persistence in the error term. Additionally, we use Prais-Winsten panel corrected standard errors to account for cross section correlation among the survey participants.

Tables 6.3 and 6.4 display the estimation results for $\rho = 0$, i.e. the case in which we do not include the feature of interest rate smoothing.[15] The first two regressions for each country are contemporaneous versions, i.e. all variables enter with the same time index. The first equation (called 'Short') regresses the three-month short-term interest rate forecast on the three-month forecasts of inflation and output growth (i.e., $l = k = q = 3$). The second regression (called 'Medium') uses twelve-month forecasts for all variables instead (i.e., $l = k = q = 12$).

For the Latin-American countries (Table 6.3) the results show that expected inflation and expected output growth are indeed significant predictors for the forecasted interest rates. Furthermore, the coefficient of the inflation rate is significantly higher than unity for Mexico while it is not significantly different from unity in the case of Brazil. This suggests that the *Taylor principle* only holds (i.e. $\alpha_1 > 1$) in economies which are classified as inflation targeting countries. In the case of Argentina and Venezuela, two non-inflation targeting countries, the inflation coefficients are instead significantly lower from what the *Taylor principle* suggests. Moreover, for Brazil (short-term), Mexico and Chile the expected output growth coefficients are also in line with our theoretical considerations and of reasonable size. In contrast, for the non-inflation targeting countries the output coefficient has the

[15] In a first step we do not allow for a smoothing effect because empirical work on Taylor rules has shown that the fit is highly dominated by this parameter. We, thus, start out with the assumption of no smoothing effect in order to study other effects first, such as the *Taylor principle*.

wrong sign which contradicts the Taylor rule. However, a significant negative sign turned out to be a strong feature in the estimation results. Fendel et al. (2007) find the same feature for expectations about the Fed behavior and refer to this as a 'reversed causality'. Forecasters only observe the ex post causality, i.e. that output growth rates react to changes in the official interest rate: If the short-term interest rate is increased output growth slows down. However, forecasters do not base their forecasts on the fact that when the central bank expects or observes higher output growth it tends to increase official interest rates due to the inflationary pressure. The latter can be referred to as the ex ante causality.

The results also hold if we allow for a forward-looking version of the Taylor rule. In the third regression (called 'Forward') we regress the three-month forecast of the short-term interest rate on the twelve-month forecasts of the output growth and the inflation rate (i.e., $l = 3$ and $k = q = 12$). While the coefficient on the inflation rate is still significantly higher than unity for Mexico, the coefficient for the output growth still has the wrong sign in the cases of Argentina and Venezuela. In order to account for the severe financial crisis in Argentina from 1998 - 2002 we also estimate regression (6.12) for Argentina for the time period January 2003 until December 2007.[16] Yet, the negative sign in the expected output development still prevails and again the *Taylor principle* remains violated. Besides that, the autoregressive parameter in the error terms is significant and ranges between 0.71 and 0.95. This basically supports our model specification.

Table 6.4 reports the corresponding results for the central and eastern European countries. The financial market expects the *Taylor principle* to hold in expectations for Poland (medium-term), while for other countries the *Taylor principle* is rejected in the expectations. Interestingly, again for non-inflation targeting countries the *Taylor rule* does not fit expectations since either the interest rate is not expected to respond to the inflation rate (Slovakia) or the output coefficient has the wrong sign (Turkey). Additionally, the auto regressive parameter is significant and ranges from 0.61 to 0.96.

In sum, the Taylor rule seems to be adopted by financial market participants in forecasting the short-term interest rate for Mexico and Poland. For Brazil the Taylor principle cannot be rejected. Thus, on the one hand in inflation targeting countries of our sample there are more or less pronounced

[16] We choose to start the curtailed sample for Argentina from 2003 onwards although we are aware that the aftermaths of the financial crisis still prevailed. The reason is that the interest rate came down from 50 percent in August 2002 to about 5.7 percent in January 2003 which is close to the post crisis long-term level of about 4.6 percent.

Table 6.3: Expected Taylor-type rule for Latin-American countries (April 2001 - December 2007)

Country		α_0	α_1	α_2	AR	R^2	Obs.	Groups
Argentina	Short	7.94*	.47*	-.60*	.71*	.98	821	27
		(.34)	(.03)	(.12)				
	Medium	7.88*	.55*	-.61*	.73*	.97	687	27
		(.31)	(.03)	(.13)				
	Forward	5.17*	.63*	-.41*	.75*	.99	755	27
		(.38)	(.04)	(.18)				
Argentina (2003 - 2007)	Short	5.04*	.33*	-.09	.91*	.98	666	22
		(.08)	(.03)	(.09)				
	Medium	3.86*	.43*	.07	.88*	.97	555	22
		(.09)	(.05)	(.08)				
	Forward	5.55*	.38*	-.24*	.93*	.98	619	22
		(.88)	(.03)	(.10)				
Brazil	Short	9.80*	1.02*	.40*	.90*	.97	1,306	30
		(.05)	(.04)	(.08)				
	Medium	9.93*	.97*	-.01	.86*	.97	1,267	30
		(.06)	(.04)	(.09)				
	Forward	11.22*	.99*	.14	.90*	.98	1,293	30
		(.05)	(.04)	(.09)				
Mexico	Short	2.86*	.96*	.24*	.86*	.97	1,298	26
		(.04)	(.06)	(.05)				
	Medium	2.37*	1.19*	.14*	.85*	.98	1,297	26
		(.32)	(.06)	(.05)				
	Forward	2.07*	1.18*	.22*	.85*	.99	1,295	26
		(.06)	(.07)	(.06)				
Venzuela	Short	14.28*	.12*	-.14*	.88*	.98	780	20
		(.17)	(.03)	(.05)				
	Medium	12.16*	.27*	-.47*	.78*	.97	716	20
		(.29)	(.04)	(.07)				
	Forward	15.56*	.12*	-.33*	.87*	.99	732	20
		(.21)	(.04)	(.07)				
Chile	Short	3.46*	.33*	.05	.95*	.98	1,228	25
		(.02)	(.03)	(.05)				
	Medium	1.17*	.69*	.34*	.92*	.99	1,199	25
		(.03)	(.06)	(.06)				
	Forward	2.46*	.55*	.12*	.95*	.98	1,211	25
		(.02)	(.05)	(.06)				

Notes: Estimated equation (6.12) $E_t i_{t+1} = (1-\rho)\alpha_0 + \alpha_1(1-\rho)E_t\pi_{t+k} + \alpha_2(1-\rho)E_t(\Delta y_{t+q}) + \rho i_t + \epsilon_t$ by the means of a serial correlation model where by the means of a serial correlation model where $\epsilon_{t,i} = \beta_i \epsilon_{t-1,i}$ (6.13) and $= \rho = 0$; values in parentheses present panel corrected standard errors applying the Prais-Winsten model; the Hausman test reflects the level of significance that the random effects estimator is appropriate, otherwise the fixed effects estimator is used; * (+) indicates significance at the one (ten) percent level, respectively.

indications that the expectation formation process can be explained by the Taylor rule. On the other hand, in all non-inflation targeting countries (i.e. in Argentina, Venezuela, Slovakia and Turkey) the expectation formation process in financial markets cannot be explained by the Taylor rule arguments. Thus, the analysis so far indicates that the adoption of inflation targeting

Table 6.4: Expected Taylor-type rule for central and eastern European countries (May 1998 - December 2007)

Country		α_0	α_1	α_2	AR	R^2	Obs.	Groups
	Short	1.54*	.39*	-.02	.92*	.96	856	24
		(.02)	(.02)	(.02)				
Czech Rep.	Medium	3.29*	.56*	-.21*	.73*	.97	848	24
		(.05)	(.03)	(.03)				
	Forward	2.10*	.43*	.00	.85*	.99	856	24
		(.02)	(.02)	(.03)				
	Short	6.59*	.38*	.15	.86*	.97	688	24
		(.07)	(.04)	(.10)				
Hungary	Medium	3.29*	.64*	.37*	.77*	.96	685	24
		(.11)	(.05)	(.09)				
	Forward	4.24*	.72*	.30*	.81*	.99	688	24
		(.10)	(.05)	(.09)				
	Short	4.18*	.82*	.21*	.89*	.99	931	29
		(.05)	(.05)	(.07)				
Poland	Medium	1.84*	1.26*	.30*	.77*	.96	923	29
		(.10)	(.05)	(.07)				
	Forward	1.94*	1.02*	.47*	.90*	.98	930	29
		(.05)	(.06)	(.08)				
	Short	-.46*	-.06	.34*	.96*	.97	528	18
		(.07)	(.06)	(.12)				
Slovakia	Medium	2.87*	-.13+	.04	.95*	.96	524	18
		(.07)	(.07)	(.12)				
	Forward	2.32*	-.14+	.08	.95*	.97	528	18
		(.07)	(.08)	(.13)				
	Short	18.34*	.70*	-1.21*	.66*	.96	719	24
		(.16)	(.03)	(.15)				
Turkey	Medium	15.22*	.63*	-.96*	.72*	.96	621	24
		(.53)	(.04)	(.25)				
	Forward	16.79*	.87*	-1.22*	.61*	.97	677	24
		(.61)	(.03)	(.22)				

Notes: Estimated equation (6.12) $E_t i_{t+1} = (1-\rho)\alpha_0 + \alpha_1(1-\rho)E_t\pi_{t+k} + \alpha_2(1-\rho)E_t(\Delta y_{t+q}) + \rho i_t + \epsilon_t$ by the means of a serial correlation model where by the means of a serial correlation model where $\epsilon_{t,i} = \beta_i \epsilon_{t-1,i}$ (6.13) and $= \rho = 0$; values in parentheses present panel corrected standard errors applying the Prais-Winsten model; the Hausman test reflects the level of significance that the random effects estimator is appropriate, otherwise the fixed effects estimator is used; * (+) indicates significance at the one (ten) percent level, respectively.

leads to a systematically different expectation formation process in financial markets.

In a next step we depart from the assumption that $\rho = 0$ and jointly estimate the smoothing parameter. Results are presented in Tables 6.5 and 6.6. We use the actual (observable) short-term interest as the quasi lagged interest rate in our regressions and apply the same timing as in the corresponding regressions from Tables 6.5 and 6.6. Thus, we test for the persistence in expectations. Not surprisingly, the results indicate that the predicted interest rate is highly dominated by the current interest rate for the inflation targeting countries as suggested by a significant smoothing parameter ranging around 0.5 to 0.9.[17] Argentina (full sample), Slovakia (medium-term and forward looking), Venezuela and Turkey experienced low interest rate persistence (ρ is smaller than 0.3) and hence, reflecting high expected changes in the interest rates during that period.

Again, the results suggest that the Taylor principle only holds (i.e. $\alpha_1 > 1$) in inflation targeting countries, namely Brazil, Chile, Mexico and Poland. For the Czech Republic the *Taylor principle* cannot be rejected in the medium-term version. Apparently, this supports our previous conclusion that inflation targeting matters for expectation formation: the *Taylor principle* if at all only holds in inflation targeting countries. The Taylor principle does not hold for Argentina, Hungary, Slovakia, Turkey, and Venezuela where the latter three are the non-inflation targeting countries. For Argentina (after excluding the period before 2003) as a non-inflation targeting country we obtain higher expected smoothing parameters of about 0.4, but still the *Taylor principle* remains violated.

With respect to the output coefficient we find again the wrong sign for all non-inflation targeting countries. While the output gap coefficient is significantly positive in the cases of Chile and Mexico, it is not significantly different from zero for Brazil, at least in the medium-term and forward looking version. Interestingly, Schmidt-Hebbel and Werner (2002) report a significant output gap coefficient for Chile estimating the central bank reaction function by the means of equation (6.12). By contrast they find an insignificant value for the output gap for Brazil which is supported by our results.

For the central and eastern European countries the sign of the output coefficient does not change substantially by introducing the smoothing feature. While we find significantly positive output coefficients for the inflation targeting countries, namely Poland and Hungary, for the non-inflation targeting countries the output coefficients are significantly negative while for the Czech Republic the coefficient is ambiguous.

---

[17]This result is in line with the stylized fact that inflation expectations are more persistent in inflation targeting countries compared to non-inflation targeting countries (Levin, Natalucci and Piger, 2004). This finding also matches the well-demonstrated phenomenon that expectations in financial markets are rather static than dynamic (Mitchell and Pearce, 2007a). Furthermore, Krueger and Kuttner (1996) found that the Federal Funds future market provide efficient predictions on the future path of the Federal Funds rate. As the future and actual path of the Federal Funds rate are close to each other, static expectations seem reasonable as a means to forecast interest rates. Furthermore, applying actual data Schmidt-Hebbel and Werner (2002) estimate the Taylor rule by means of equation (6.12)

Table 6.5: Expected Taylor-type rule for Latin-American countries and interest rate smoothing (April 2001 - December 2007)

Country		α_0	α_1	α_2	ρ	AR	R^2	Obs.	Groups
Argentina	Short	5.34*	.54*	-.45*	.16*	.77*	.00	815	27
		(.30)	(.04)	(.15)	(.02)				
	Medium	7.49*	.56*	-.64*	.07*	.74*	.00	682	27
		(.33)	(.04)	(.15)	(.02)				
	Forward	1.49*	.77*	-.13*	.17*	.80*	.58	749	27
		(.33)	(.05)	(.22)	(.02)				
Argentina (2003 - 2007)	Short	1.76*	.53*	-.09	.46*	.88*	56	644	22
		(.10)	(.07)	(.15)	(.05)				
	Medium	1.70*	.55*	.16	.33*	.84*	.20	555	22
		(.11)	(.07)	(.12)	(.05)				
	Forward	1.60*	.45*	-.00	.43*	.90*	.99	597	22
		(.09)	(.07)	(.15)	(.05)				
Brazil	Short	1.56*	1.59*	.46+	.71*	.76*	.02	1,306	30
		(.09)	(.10)	(.19)	(.02)				
	Medium	4.74*	.99*	-.16	.49*	.82*	.25	1,267	30
		(.08)	(.06)	(.14)	(.03)				
	Forward	2.07*	1.65*	-.19	.73*	.75*	.45	1,293	30
		(.09)	(.11)	(.25)	(.02)				
Mexico	Short	.76*	1.37*	.21*	.53*	.65*	.00	1,298	26
		(.07)	(.09)	(.06)	(.02)				
	Medium	1.34*	1.30*	.20*	.28*	.76*	.00	1,271	26
		(.06)	(.08)	(.06)	(.02)				
	Forward	.50*	1.49*	.26*	.52*	.64*	.00	1,295	26
		(.08)	(.10)	(.08)	(.02)				
Venzuela	Short	13.55*	.14*	-.16*	.05+	.85*	.00	780	20
		(.19)	(.03)	(.05)	(.02)				
	Medium	11.50*	.28*	-.46*	.04	.76*	.00	716	20
		(.32)	(.04)	(.07)	(.02)				
	Forward	14.58*	.14*	-.32*	.04+	.85*	.00	732	20
		(.23)	(.04)	(.08)	(.02)				
Chile	Short	-.43*	1.40*	.87*	.88*	.36*	.00	1,228	25
		(.05)	(.15)	(.14)	(.01)				
	Medium	-.46*	1.39*	.62*	.66*	.66*	.00	1,199	25
		(.06)	(.12)	(.10)	(.02)				
	Forward	-.75*	2.02*	.92*	.87*	.36*	.00	1,211	25
		(.06)	(.20)	(.15)	(.01)				

Notes: Estimated equation (6.12) $E_t i_{t+1} = (1-\rho)\alpha_0 + \alpha_1(1-\rho)E_t\pi_{t+k} + \alpha_2(1-\rho)E_t(\Delta y_{t+q}) + \rho i_t + \epsilon_t$ by the means of a serial correlation model where by the means of a serial correlation model where $\epsilon_{t,i} = \beta_i \epsilon_{t-1,i}$ (6.13); values in parentheses present panel corrected standard errors applying the Prais-Winsten model; the Hausman test reflects the level of significance that the random effects estimator is appropriate, otherwise the fixed effects estimator is used; * (+) indicates significance at the one (ten) percent level, respectively.

In sum, the inspection of Tables 6.5 and 6.6 suggests that the Taylor-type rules seem to explain the forecasts very well for the majority of inflation targeting countries once we allow for interest rate smoothing while this conclusion does not hold for non-inflation targeting countries.

---

for Brazil, Chile and Mexico. They find smoothing coefficients similar to ours for Brazil, Chile and Mexico of about 0.83, 0.96 and 0.62, respectively.

Table 6.6: Expected Taylor-type rule for central and eastern European countries and interest rate smoothing (May 1998 - December 2007)

Country		α_0	α_1	α_2	ρ	AR	R^2	Obs.	Groups
	Short	.33*	.58*	-.07	.90*	.00	.99	856	24
		(.04)	(.08)	(.10)	(.01)				
Czech Rep.	Medium	.76*	.45*	.23	.84*	.00	.94	848	24
		(.06)	(.15)	(.17)	(.03)				
	Forward	.20*	.90*	-.03	.89*	.25	.99	856	24
		(.04)	(.09)	(.11)	(.01)				
	Short	.26+	.30*	1.01*	.83*	.00	.94	688	24
		(.10)	(.11)	(.24)	(.02)				
Hungary	Medium	.46*	.39*	.52*	.65*	.00	.87	685	24
		(.11)	(.10)	(.17)	(.03)				
	Forward	.33*	.70*	.56*	.78*	.00	.95	688	24
		(.10)	(.09)	(.19)	(.02)				
	Short	-.12*	1.13*	.80*	.89*	.36	.99	931	29
		(.06)	(.14)	(.27)	(.02)				
Poland	Medium	-.11	.26*	1.04*	.77*	.00	.96	923	29
		(.09)	(.18)	(.21)	(.02)				
	Forward	-.33*	1.32*	1.01*	.89*	.04	.99	930	29
		(.07)	(.16)	(.31)	(.02)				
	Short	1.59*	.38+	-.60+	.79*	.00	.91	528	18
		(.40)	(.18)	(.27)	(.02)				
Slovakia	Medium	4.20*	-.08	-.01	.11*	.00	.69	524	18
		(.08)	(.07)	(.13)	(.02)				
	Forward	3.27*	-.01	.03	.29*	.00	.91	528	18
		(.08)	(.09)	(.15)	(.02)				
	Short	13.83*	.65*	-1.47*	.28*	.00	.88	719	24
		(.51)	(.04)	(.19)	(.03)				
Turkey	Medium	10.94*	.63*	-1.07*	.15*	.00	.78	645	24
		(1.85)	(.04)	(.30)	(.03)				
	Forward	13.01*	.85*	-1.37*	.23*	.00	.90	677	24
		(.65)	(.03)	(.27)	(.03)				

Notes: Estimated equation (6.12) $E_t i_{t+1} = (1-\rho)\alpha_0 + \alpha_1(1-\rho)E_t\pi_{t+k} + \alpha_2(1-\rho)E_t(\Delta y_{t+q}) + \rho i_t + \epsilon_t$ by the means of a serial correlation model where by the means of a serial correlation model where $\epsilon_{t,i} = \beta_i \epsilon_{t-1,i}$ (6.13); values in parentheses present panel corrected standard errors applying the Prais-Winsten model; the Hausman test reflects the level of significance that the random effects estimator is appropriate, otherwise the fixed effects estimator is used; * (+) indicates significance at the one (ten) percent level, respectively.

The estimation procedure so far allows us to investigate another feature inherent in the Taylor rule. Equation (6.12) allows us to calculate the long-term inflation rate expected by the financial market (π^*). In order to recover the expected inflation target π^* we can use the parameter estimates α_0 and α_1 from Table 6.5 and 6.6. Recall that

$$\alpha_0 = \bar{i} - \alpha_1 E_t \pi^* \qquad (6.11)$$

and given the Fisher relation

$$(6.14) \qquad \bar{i} = i^{real} + E(\pi^*)$$

which together yields

$$\alpha_0 = i^{real} + (1 - \alpha_1)E_t\pi^*. \tag{6.15}$$

This implies that

$$E_t\pi^* = \frac{\alpha_0 - i^{real}}{1 - \alpha_1}. \tag{6.16}$$

According to Clarida et al. (1998) we can use the expected sample average real interest rate among all individuals to provide an estimate of i^{real} as our sample is sufficiently long. With these estimates it is possible to construct the expected inflation target rate $Et(\pi^*)$ by the means of the short-term results shown in Table 6.5 and 6.6 reflecting the estimation of equation (6.12).

The expected real interest rate, the long-term inflation rate and the actual inflation rate are shown in Table 6.7. The expected long-term inflation rate is the highest for Turkey amounting to 47 percent on an annual basis. Indeed, with a rate of 31 percent annually Turkey experienced the highest inflation rate in our sample. The expected inflation rate which underlies the Taylor rule is also very close to the actual inflation rate for Argentina (21.7 compared to 17.8 percent), Brazil (9.4 compared to 7.8 percent), Mexico (5.3 compared to 4.4 percent), Venezuela (25.6 compared to 18.5 percent), Slovakia (10.6 compared to 6.1 percent) and the Czech Republic (5.4 compared to 3.2 percent). Although, the actual and the expected inflation rate are close to each other, there remains a huge difference at least for Chile, Hungary and Poland. Before jumping on the conclusion that the financial market provides inaccurate expectations one has to recall that the Taylor rule estimated in our analysis is based on expectations which might not coincide with the realized inflation rate. Hence, we should not blame the financial market for adopting a higher long-term inflation rate compared to the actual one. Moreover it seems possible, if not likely, that the financial market learns during the inflation process and the assumption of a constant long-term inflation rate might not be appropriate. Therefore the next section accounts for the possibility of a time-variant long-term inflation rate.

6.5 The role of time-varying inflation targets and credibility

In this section we analyze the link between expected interest rates, projected output development and inflation rate forecasts in more detail by allowing

Table 6.7: Expected long-term inflation targets (E[π^*]) and actual inflation rates

Period April 2001 - Dec. 2007	Argentina	Brazil	Chile	Mexico	Venezuela
Expected Real Interest Rate	-3.6	10.8	0.9	3.6	-7.9
Expected Inflation Rate	21.7	9.4	11.3	5.3	25.6
Actual Average Inflation Rate	17.8	7.8	2.7	4.4	18.5

Period May 1998 - Dec. 2007	Czech Rep.	Hungary	Poland	Slovakia	Turkey
Expected Real Interest Rate	0.9	2.6	5.0	1.2	3.0
Expected Inflation Rate	5.4	-1.6	47.1	10.6	47.2
Actual Average Inflation Rate	3.2	7.0	3.9	6.1	31.2

Notes: Expected real interest rates reflect the average expected real interest rate over the respective sample period; the expected inflation rate is calculated by the means of (6.16) $E_t\pi^* = \frac{\alpha_0 - i^{real}}{1-\alpha_1}$ and the estimation results of Table 6.5 and 6.6; the actual inflation rate reflects the average inflation rate as displayed in Tables 6.1 and 6.2; the sources of the actual inflation rate are presented in Tables 6.1 and 6.2.

for a time-varying inflation target. As our sample consists of six inflation targeting countries (Brazil, Chile, Mexico, Poland, Hungary and the Czech Republic) which publicly announce inflation targets we now incorporate the time variance of the official inflation target into our analysis. The inflation targets are obtained from the monthly inflation reports of the respective central bank. Figures 6.1 to 6.6 show the inflation target (thick solid line), the mean of the six-months expected inflation rate $\bar{E}_t[\pi_{t+1}]$ (dotted line) and the actual inflation rate (solid line). Not surprisingly, the expected and the actual inflation rate move in line. This feature can be attributed to the fact that the financial market uses the actual inflation rate as a benchmark to build inflation expectations. Figures 6.1 to 6.6 also show that the inflation target in the cases of the Latin-American countries is relatively stable compared to the cental and eastern European countries. Notwithstanding, we now take the feature of the time-varying inflation target into account and analyze whether the financial market treats the long-term inflation rate π^* to be time-invariant.[18]

[18] Since the Czech Republic and Hungary introduced the inflation targeting system in June 1999 and December 2001, respectively, we drop all observations prior to this date.

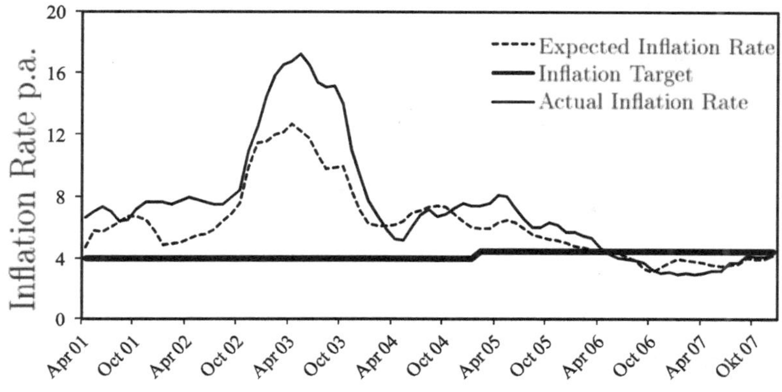

Figure 6.1: Inflation target, expected and actual inflation rate in Brazil

Note: Figure 6.1 shows the inflation target (thick solid line), the mean of the six-months expected inflation rate

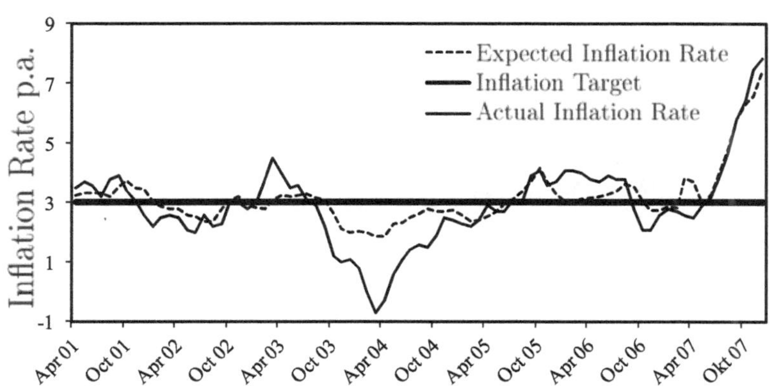

Figure 6.2: Inflation target, expected and actual inflation rate in Chile

Note: Figure 6.2 shows the inflation target (thick solid line), the mean of the six-months expected inflation rate $\bar{E}_t[\pi_{t+1}]$ (dotted line) and the actual inflation rate (solid line) at time t.

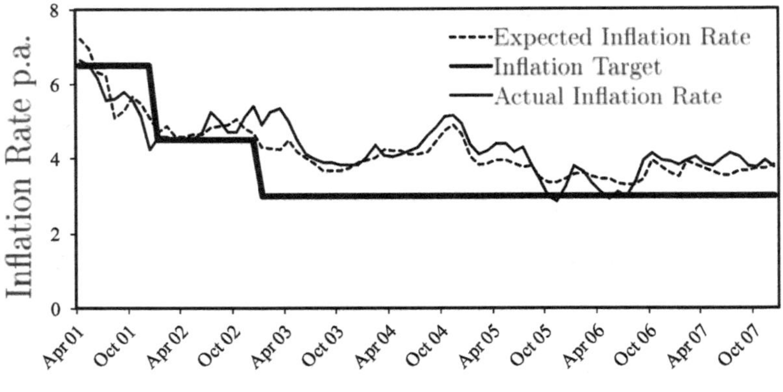

Figure 6.3: Inflation target, expected and actual inflation rate in Mexico

Note: Figure 6.3 shows the inflation target (thick solid line), the mean of the six-months expected inflation rate $\bar{E}_t[\pi_{t+1}]$ (dotted line) and the actual inflation rate (solid line) at time t.

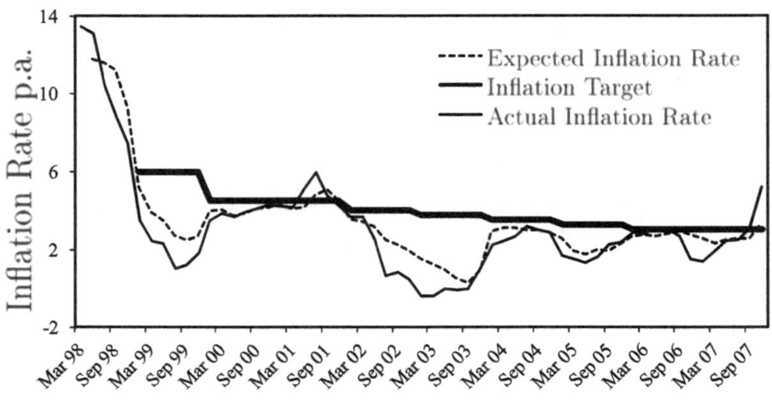

Figure 6.4: Inflation target, expected and actual inflation rate in the Czech Republic

Note: Figure 6.4 shows the inflation target (thick solid line), the mean of the six-months expected inflation rate $\bar{E}_t[\pi_{t+1}]$ (dotted line) and the actual inflation rate (solid line) at time t.

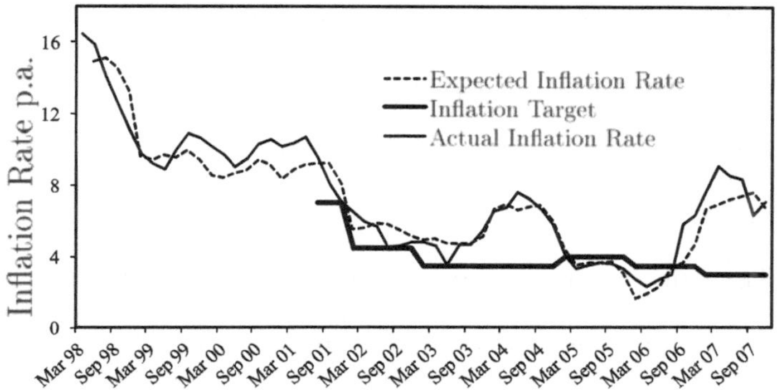

Figure 6.5: Inflation target, expected and actual inflation rate in Hungary

Note: Figure 6.5 shows the inflation target (thick solid line), the mean of the six-months expected inflation rate $\bar{E}_t[\pi_{t+1}]$ (dotted line) and the actual inflation rate (solid line) at time t.

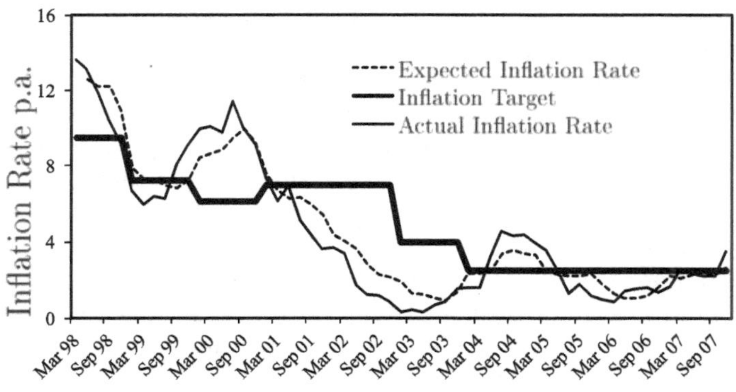

Figure 6.6: Inflation target, expected and actual inflation rate in Poland

Note: Figure 6.6 shows the inflation target (thick solid line), the mean of the six-months expected inflation rate $\bar{E}_t[\pi_{t+1}]$ (dotted line) and the actual inflation rate (solid line) at time t.

Starting from equation (6.9) we now treat the inflation target as observable but time-varying and, thus, do not need to include it in the constant. Therefore we depart from the former specification (6.12) and estimate[19]

$$(6.17)\quad E_t i_{t+l} = (1-\rho)\alpha_0 + \alpha_1(1-\rho)E_t(\pi_{t+k}-\pi^*) + \alpha_2(1-\rho)E_t(\Delta y_{t+q}) + \rho i_t + \epsilon_t$$

$$with\ \ \alpha_0 = \bar{i}.$$

The estimation results are presented in Table 6.8 and 6.9. Compared to Table 6.5 and 6.6 (constant implicit inflation target) the results do not change for Brazil, Chile and the Czech Republic. This is due to the fact that these countries did not change their targets substantially during the observation period. For the remaining three inflation targeting countries, significant differences between the specifications of the time-constant (Tables 6.5 and 6.6) and time-varying inflation targets (Tables 6.8 and 6.9) emerge. For Mexico the *Taylor principle* no longer holds as the inflation coefficient is insignificant (short- and medium-term version) or has even the wrong sign (forward looking version). This means that the financial market does not expect the Central Bank of Mexico to respond to inflation changes in the direction suggested by the Taylor rule including the announced inflation target as the long-term inflation rate. An interpretation of this finding is that financial market participants do not trust the official announced inflation targets in case of Mexico compared to Brazil and Chile. This confirms the results of Schmidt-Hebbel and Werner (2002) analyzing the credibility of the inflation targeting of these three countries. Their results suggest that, in the case of Mexico, a substantial deviation exists between actual and expected inflation, whereas this is not found in the cases of Brazil and Chile. The authors also find substantial deviations of the inflation target from the expected inflation rate which supports our previous finding according to which the incorporation of the inflation target is not being reflected in the expectations of the financial market.

Although Hungary has been changing the target quite frequently, the results do not change with respect to the market forecasts in the Taylor rule framework. The output coefficient still has the expected sign, while the *Taylor principle* remains violated. For Poland the *Taylor principle* can only be rejected in the medium-term specification and the output coefficient is still significantly positive.

[19] Since we learned from the previous analysis that interest rate smoothing is crucial for the analysis we jointly estimate the smoothing parameter and refrain from the assumption that $\rho = 0$.

Table 6.8: Application with interest rate smoothing and time-varying inflation target (April 2001 - December 2007)

Country	Brazil			Mexico			Chile		
Horizon	Short	Med.	Forw.	Short	Med.	Forw.	Short	Med.	Forw.
$(1-\rho)\alpha_0$	2.44*	5.66*	2.74*	2.52*	3.98*	2.33*	-.02	.30*	-.13
	(.09)	(.09)	(.10)	(.07)	(.06)	(.19)	(.05)	(.05)	(.09)
$(1-\rho)\alpha_1$	.39*	.43*	.36*	.00	-.03	-.09+	.17*	.42*	.30*
	(.04)	(.04)	(.04)	(.05)	(.05)	(.04)	(.02)	(.05)	(.03)
$(1-\rho)\alpha_2$	.18*	-.02	.04	-.00	.19*	-.04	.12*	.32*	.15*
	(.06)	(.08)	(.07)	(.04)	(.05)	(.05)	(.01)	(.03)	(.02)
ρ	.78*	.52*	.80*	.70*	.42*	.74*	.89*	.71*	.88*
	(.02)	(.02)	(.02)	(.02)	(.03)	(.17)	(.01)	(.02)	(.01)
AR	.77*	.82*	.75*	.60*	.75*	.60*	.36*	.66*	.36*
R^2 within	.70	.49	.73	.49	.23	.79	.89	.63	.93
R^2 between	.97	.86	.97	.51	.21	.78	.98	.77	.99
R^2 overall	.87	.69	.87	.71	.46	.78	.94	.81	.93
α_1	1.72*	.90*	1.76*	.01	-.05	-.36+	1.56*	1.46*	2.50*
Chi^2-Test	(.15)	(.08)	(.16)	(.16)	(.09)	(.17)	(.18)	(.17)	(.25)
$\alpha_1 = 1$	.00	.20	.00	.00	.00	.00	.00	.00	.00
α_2	.82*	-.05	.18	.01	.34*	-.16	1.08*	1.12*	1.24*
Chi^2-Test	(.26)	(.18)	(.34)	(.12)	(.08)	(.18)	(.16)	(.11)	(.18)
$\alpha_1 = 0$	.00	.79	.59	.95	.00	.10	.00	.00	.00
Hausman	.00	.00	.00	.00	.00	.47	.00	.00	.48
Obs.	1,306	1,267	1,293	1,298	1,271	1,321	1,228	1,199	1,236
Groups	30	30	30	26	26	26	25	25	25

Notes: Estimated equation (6.17) $E_t i_{t+1} = (1-\rho)\alpha_0 + \alpha_1(1-\rho)E_t\pi_{t+k} + \alpha_2(1-\rho)E_t(\Delta y_{t+q}) + \rho i_t + \epsilon_t$ by the means of a serial correlation model where $\epsilon_{t,i} = \beta_i \epsilon_{t-1,i}$ (6.13); values in parentheses present panel corrected standard errors applying the Prais-Winsten model; the Hausman test reflects the level of significance that the random effects estimator is appropriate, otherwise the fixed effects estimator is used; the Chi^2 tests whether the Taylor principle holds (i.e. $\alpha_1 > 1$); * (+) indicates significance at the one (ten) percent level, respectively.

An additional feature for Mexico is revealed by comparing Tables 6.5 and 6.8. We find an increase of the smoothing parameter from about 0.5 to 0.7 for the short-term (forward looking) version and from 0.3 to 0.4 for the medium-term version. This means that the financial market again expects the Mexican central bank to change its interest rates to a lesser extent in the specification with the inflation target announcement. Put differently, the persistence of the expected short-term interest rate reflects that the financial market does not trust the Mexican central bank to respond to inflation

Table 6.9: Application with interest rate smoothing and time-varying inflation target (May 1998 - December 2007)

Country	Czech Republic			Hungary			Poland		
Horizon	Short	Med.	Forw.	Short	Med.	Forw.	Short	Med.	Forw.
$(1\text{-}\rho)\alpha_0$	.26*	.83*	.19+	.38*	1.08*	.54*	.09	-.26+	-.10
	(.08)	(.17)	(.09)	(.13)	(.12)	(.13)	(.09)	(.11)	(.09)
$(1\text{-}\rho)\alpha_1$	.05*	.04	.05*	.08*	.09*	.15*	.08*	-.03	.08*
	(.01)	(.03)	(.01)	(.03)	(.04)	(.03)	(.02)	(.03)	(.02)
$(1\text{-}\rho)\alpha_2$	.01	.01	.02+	.29*	.35*	.27*	.06+	.27*	.09*
	(.01)	(.03)	(.01)	(.06)	(.08)	(.06)	(.03)	(.04)	(.03)
ρ	.95*	.89*	.95*	.78*	.58*	.76*	.94*	.80*	.94*
	(.01)	(.17)	(.01)	(.02)	(.03)	(.02)	(.01)	(.01)	(.01)
AR	.44*	.52*	.45*	.45*	.63*	.44*	.50*	.55*	.49*
R^2 within	.96	.88	.96	.84	.65	.85	.96	.88	.96
R^2 between	.99	.88	.99	.91	.53	.91	.99	.98	.99
R^2 overall	.97	.86	.97	.89	.68	.90	.99	.96	.99
α_1	.93*	.34	1.08*	.38*	.22+	.64*	1.34*	-.13	1.46*
Chi^2-Test	(.21)	(.27)	(.27)	(.10)	(.09)	(.11)	(.34)	(.16)	(.41)
$\alpha_1 = 1$	.72	.00	.76	.00	.00	.00	.30	.00	.26
α_2	.23	.07	.47	1.33*	.84*	1.15*	1.05+	1.32*	1.69*
Chi^2-Test	(.23)	(.27)	(.36)	(.25)	(.18)	(.24)	(.49)	(.22)	(.58)
$\alpha_1 = 0$	.32	.80	.19	.00	.00	.00	.03	.00	.00
Hausman	.92	.35	.35	.00	.00	.00	.00	.00	.00
Obs.	579	575	579	469	466	469	931	923	930
Groups	23	23	23	23	23	23	29	29	29

Notes: Estimated equation (6.17) $E_t i_{t+1} = (1-\rho)\alpha_0 + \alpha_1(1-\rho)E_t\pi_{t+k} + \alpha_2(1-\rho)E_t(\Delta y_{t+q}) + \rho i_t + \epsilon_t$ by the means of a serial correlation model where $\epsilon_{t,i} = \beta_i \epsilon_{t-1,i}$ (6.13); values in parentheses present panel corrected standard errors applying the Prais-Winsten model; the Hausman test reflects the level of significance that the random effects estimator is appropriate, otherwise the fixed effects estimator is used; the Chi^2 tests whether the Taylor principle holds (i.e. $\alpha_1 > 1$); * (+) indicates significance at the one (ten) percent level, respectively.

changes in the specification of the time-varying inflation target.

Compared to the specification with the time-invariant inflation rate the output coefficient for the Mexican case is now positive only in the medium-term version. Recall that in the short-term and forward-looking version with a time-constant inflation target, the output coefficient has the expected positive sign and is both significant and of reasonable magnitude. Also the fit suffers in the case of Mexico, when incorporating the inflation target as the time-varying long-term inflation rate which reflects that the estimation of a time-constant inflation target is superior. In sum, the financial market does not incorporate the announced inflation target of the Central Bank of Mexico in forecasts of the short-term interest rate by the means of the Taylor rule. However, the Taylor rule works when we assume that the financial market expects constant a long-term inflation rate that is different to the inflation target. Apparently the Central Bank of Mexico does not seem to be credible in the eyes of the financial market to reduce the inflation rate. This feature is also reflected in the statement of the Central Bank of Mexico (2004, p.45) that "both the level of total core CPI inflation and its expectations suggest that the 3 percent inflation target has still not been included in a widespread fashion into the price determination process." By contrast, the announcements of the inflation target of the central banks of Brazil, Chile, Hungary and the Czech Republic seem to be regarded as being credible as the results do not change when including the inflation target into the baseline model while the results do change in case of Poland.

6.6 Conclusion

This chapter investigates whether the adoption of inflation targeting matters for the expectation formation process in the financial market. Using survey data of the CEF we analyze whether the financial market predicts short-term interest rates in the basis of the Taylor rule for five Latin-American countries and five central and eastern European countries. We find that for most inflation targeting countries financial markets adopt the Taylor rule at least at some time horizon and provide interest rate forecasts close to the realized interest rate. These economies are Brazil, Chile, Mexico, Poland, and the Czech Republic. Only Hungary seems to be an exception among the group of inflation targeting economies. Compared to that, for non-inflation targeting countries the financial market does not adopt the Taylor rule which is in every case reflected in the violation of the *Taylor principle.*

We also included a time-varying inflation target which is the announced inflation target for the inflation targeting countries. The results indicate that for Brazil, Chile, Poland and the Czech Republic the short-term interest rate forecasts are provided by means of the Taylor rule whereas for Mexico the Taylor rule is now violated. Apparently, for Mexico the financial market incorporates a long-term inflation rate that is different to the announced inflation target rate.

Chapter 7

Conclusion and policy implications

This thesis investigates the expectation formation process in financial markets by the means of survey data. Compared to an ex-post analysis which analyzes the actual market outcome, survey data allow to directly examine the expectation formation process. Therefore, survey data analysis is referred to as an ex-ante analysis which is superior compared to an ex-post analysis[1]. The thesis focuses on the two major financial markets in terms of trading volume, namely the foreign exchange market and the money market. Both markets can be regarded as highly liquid and information efficient.[2] The aim of this thesis is to analyze, first, how expectations are formed in financial markets in principle. We find that exchange rate expectation are formed irrationally which means that market participants do not use all available information to forecast financial and real economy variables. Moreover, assuming a distributed lag model, we find that long-term foreign exchange forecasts do not correspond to the composite short-term forecasts. This is referred to as inconsistent expectations.[3] Second, the thesis provides evidence

[1]This is the case when when unexpected events, such as exogenous shocks occur. If the ex-post analysis dies not control for the exogenous shock then the estimation results are biased. Compared to that the ex-ante analysis circumvents this problem which also occurs when expected events did not take place.

[2]The latter refers to the fact that market participants have equal access to information. This does, however, neither imply that each and every market participant uses the same information set or applies the same model to form its expectations. Nor do we assume that expectations are formed rational

[3]Since consistency compared to rationality does not require expectations to match a stochastic process generating actual exchange rates, it is a weaker and, therefore, neces-

that financial market participants are heterogeneous in the way that financial market participants do not use the same model to build their expectations. However, our analysis shows that there exists two different groups of foreign exchange traders, namely those using a stabilizing and other using a destabilizing expectation model. Accounting for this core results the thesis develops a microstructural framework in which both groups interact simultaneously. Within this framework we show that the central bank effectively manage the exchange rate when misalignments of the exchange rate are generated by non-fundamental (destabilizing) influences. Moreover, we provide empirical evidence that the intervention policy of the Reserve Bank of Australia (RBA) act as a coordinating signal by encouraging stabilizing speculators to re-enter the market, and thereby providing a rationale for the RBA's ongoing intervention policy.

The thesis also focuses on expectation formation process in the money market. More precisely, we investigate whether financial market adopts Taylor-type rules to forecast short-term interest rates. We provide strong evidence that this is indeed the case for the G7 countries. Additionally, we show that the financial market even adopted before the Taylor rule was developed. This implies that the financial market expects the central bank to set the short-term interest rate in line with the Taylor rule although the theoretical link was not been established by the academia. Since the empirical analysis shows that the G7 central banks, indeed, apply Taylor-type rules to set the short-term interest rate (Clarida et al., 1998), we take this as evidence for a close link between the academia and the financial market. Analyzing the expectation formation process in the money market for ten emerging markets we find that expectations are formed differently under alternative monetary policy regimes. While we find that the financial market adopts Taylor-type rules for countries which introduced an inflation targeting system, we can soundly reject that Taylor-type rules are applied to non-inflation targeting countries. Moreover, we provide evidence that the inflation target is not been included in financial market forecasts in case of Mexico. This leads us to conclude that the financial market does not regard the inflation target as a credible benchmark for the monetary policy ruled out by the central bank of Mexico.[4]

This thesis is addressed to financial market participants, policy makers and the academia a like. The analysis of expectations in financial markets is

sary condition for rational expectations. Hence, rationality does require consistency, but consistency does not require rationality.

[4]Even the central bank of Mexico itself declares that inflation expectations do not account for the officially announced inflation target.

especially appealing for policy makers since they use financial market expectations to evaluate their policy actions.[5] Moreover, investigating the expectation formation process of financial market participants provides evidence which might be interesting if not useful for financial market participants itself.[6] Finally, the academia might be interested in understanding how expectations are built in financial markets and to which extent expectations are formed rational. The results of our analysis are useful for academics trying to model the financial market behavior. In sum, this thesis provides confidence that the financial market, indeed, listens what is taught in economics.

[5]For instance, since central banks are aware that their policy actions only work on real economic variables with a certain time lag most central banks react to expectations rather than to actual changes.

[6]For instance, comparing the expected and the actual exchange rate process we show that the forecast accuracy in the dollar/euro market was significantly lower for market participants forming stabilizing expectations.

Bibliography

Ahdi Noomen A., Ahmed, Gorbel and Trabelsi Abdelwahed (2003), The Reserve Bank of Australia Intervention: Exchange Rate Volatility from FI-GARCH Modelling, High Institute of Management BESTMOD Working Paper No. 03 - 02.

Allen, Helen and Mark P. Taylor (1990), Charts, Noise and Fundamentals in the London Foreign Exchange Market, *Economics Journal* 100 (400), pp. 49 - 59.

Andrew, Robert and John Broadbent (1994), Reserve Bank Operations in the Foreign Exchange Market: Effectiveness and Profitability, Research Discussion Paper 9406, Reserve Bank of Australia.

Arellano, Manuel and Stephen Bond (1991), Some Tests of Specification for Panel Data: Monte Carlo Evidence and an Application to Employment Equations, *The Review of Economic Studies* 58, pp. 277 - 297.

Audretsch, David B. and Georg Stadtmann (2005), Biases in FX-Forecasts: Evidence from Panel Data, *Global Finance Journal* 16, pp. 99 - 111.

Bank of International Settlement (2007), Triennial Central Bank Survey of Foreign Exchange and Derivatives Market Activity, Basle.

Batchelor, Roy and Pami Dua (1990), Forecaster Ideology, Forecasting Technique, and the Accuracy of Economic Forecasts, *International Journal of Forecasting* 6, pp. 3 - 10.

Beck, Roland (2001), Do Country Fundamentals Explain Emerging Market Bond Spreads?, Discussion Paper No. 2001/02, Center for Financial Studies.

Becker, Chris and Michael Sinclair (2004), Profitability of Reserve Bank Foreign Exchange Operations: Twenty Years After the Float, Research Discussion Paper 2004-06, Reserve Bank of Australia.

Benassy-Quere, Agnes, Larribeau, Sophie and Ronald MacDonald (2003), Models of Exchange Rate Expectations: How Much Heterogeneity?, *Journal of International Financial Markets, Institutions and Money* 13 (2), pp. 113 - 136.

Bollerslev, Tim and Jeffrey M. Wooldrigde (1992), Quasi Maximum likelihood Estimation and Inference in Dynamic Models with Time Varying Covariances, *Econometric Review* 11, pp. 143 - 172.

Bonham, Carl S., Cohen, Richard and Shigeyuki, Abe (2006), The Rationality and Heterogeneity of Survey Forecasts of the Yen/Dollar Exchange Rate: A Reexamination, Working Paper No. 06-11, University of Hawaii at Manoa.

Brito, Ricardo D. and Brianne Bystedt (2006), The Macroeconomic Effects of Inflation Targeting in Latin-America, Ibmec Working Paper.

Brock, William A. and Cars H. Hommes (1997), A Rational Route to Randomness, *Econometrica* 23, pp. 377 - 400.

Cavaglia, Stefano, Verschoor, Willem F. C. and Christian C. P. Wolff (1993), Further Evidence on Exchange Rate Expectations, *Journal of International Money and Finance* 12 (1), pp. 78 - 98.

Cavaglia, Stefano, Verschoor, Willem F. C. and Christian C. P. Wolff (1994), On the Biasedness of Forward Foreign Exchange Rates: Irrationality or Risk Premia?, *Journal of Business* 67 (3), pp. 321 - 343.

Central Bank of Argentina, *Inflation Report*, various issues.

Central Bank of Brazil, *Boletim do Banco Central do Brasil*, various issues.

Central Bank of Mexico, *Inflation Report*, various issues.

Cho, Dong W., and Philip L. Hersch (1998), Forecaster Characteristics and Forecast Outcomes, *Journal of Economics and Business* 50, pp. 39 - 48.

Clarida, Richard, Jordi Galí, and Mark Gertler (1998), Monetary Policy Rules in Practice: Some International Evidence, *European Economic Review* 42 (6), pp. 1033 - 1067.

Clarida, Richard, Jordi Galí, and Mark Gertler (2000), Monetary Policy and Macroeconomic Stability: Evidence and Some Theory, *The Quarterly Journal of Economics* 115 (1), pp. 147 - 166.

Corbo, Vittorio, Landerrechte, Oscar and Klaus Schmidt-Hebbel (2002), Does Inflation Targeting Make a Difference?, in: Loayza, Norman and Raimundo Soto (ed.), Inflation Targeting: Design, Performance, Challenges, pp. 221 - 269.

Corbo, Vittorio and Klaus Schmidt-Hebbel (2001), Inflation Targeting in Latin America, Central Bank of Chile Working Paper N° 105.

De Grauwe, Paul and Marianna Grimaldi (2001), Exchange Rates, Process and Money: a Long-Run Perspective, *International Journal of Finance and Economics* 6 (4), pp. 289 - 314.

De Grauwe, Paul and Marianna Grimaldi (2005), Heterogeneity of Agents and the Exchange Rate: A Nonlinear Approach, in: De Grauwe, Paul (ed.), Exchange Rate Economics: Where Do We Stand?, Cambridge and London: MIT Press, pp. 125 - 167.

De Grauwe, Paul and Marianna Grimaldi (2006), Exchange Rate Puzzles: A Tale of Switching Attractors, *European Economic Review* 50, pp. 1 - 33.

DeLong, J. Bradford, Shleifer, Andrei, Summers, Lawrence H. and Robert J. Waldmann (1990a), Noise Trader Risk in Financial Markets, *Journal of Political Economy* 98 (4), pp. 703 - 738.

DeLong, J. Bradford, Shleifer, Andrei, Summers, Lawrence H. and Robert J. Waldmann (1990b), Positive Feedbacks, Investment Strategies and Destabilizing Rational Speculation, *The Journal of Finance* 45, pp. 379 - 395.

Dominguez, Kathryn M. (1986), Are Foreign Exchange Forecasts Rational? - New Evidence from Survey Data, *Economic Letters* 21 (3), pp. 277 - 281.

Dominguez, Kathryn M. (2003), The Market Microstructure of Central Bank Intervention, *Journal of International Economics* 59, pp. 25 - 45.

Dominguez, Kathryn M. and Jeffrey A. Frankel (1993), Does Foreign Exchange Intervention Work?, Institute for International Economics, Washington.

Dornbusch, Rudiger (1976), Expectations and Exchange Rate Dynamics, *Journal of Political Economy* 84 (6), pp. 1161 - 1176.

Dutt, Swarna D. (1994), Theoretical and Empirical Analysis of Consistency in the Exchange Rate Expectation Formation Process, *Journal of Economic Integration* 9 (3), pp. 370 - 392.

Edison, Hali, Cashin, Paul and Hong Liang (2006), Foreign Exchange Intervention and the Australian Dollar: Has It Mattered?, *International Journal of Finance and Economics*, 11 (2), pp. 155 - 171.

Eisenbeis, Robert, Daniel Waggoner and Tao Zha (2002), Evaluating Wall Street Journal Survey Forecasters: A Multivariate Approach, *Business Economics* 37 (3), pp. 11 - 21.

Eitrheim, Øyvind and Timo Teräsvirta (1996), Testing the Adequacy of Smooth Transition Autoregressive Models, *Journal of Econometrics* 74 (11), pp. 59 - 75.

Elliott, Graham and Takatoshi Ito (1999), Heterogeneous Expectations and Tests of Efficiency in the Yen/Dollar Forward Exchange Rate Market, *Journal of Monetary Economics* 43, pp. 435 - 456.

Elliott, Graham, Komunjer, Ivana and Alan Timmermann (2005a), Biases in Macroeconomic Forecasts: Irrationality or Asymmetric Loss, Mimeo, UCSD.

Elliott, Graham, Komunjer, Ivana and Alan Timmermann (2005b), Estimation and Testing of Forecast Rationality under Flexible Loss, *Review of Economic Studies* 72, pp. 1107 - 1125.

Evans, Martin D. and Richard K. Lyons (2002), Order Flow and Exchange Rate Dynamics, *Journal of Political Economy* 110, pp. 170 - 180.

Fabozzi, Frank J. (2001), Handbook of Portfolio Management, New York: John Wiley and Sons.

Federal Reserve Bank (2006), Treasury and Federal Reserve Foreign Operations, several issues.

Fendel, Ralf, Frenkel, Michael and Jan-Christoph Rülke (2007), Does the Financial Market Trust in Taylor Rules? - Evidence from the WSJ Poll, Deutsche Bundesbank Discussion Paper, forthcoming.

Frankel, Jeffrey A. and Kenneth Froot (1987a), Using Survey Data to Test Standard Propositions Regarding Exchange Rate Expectations, *The American Economic Review* 77, pp. 133-153.

Frankel, Jeffrey A. and Kenneth Froot (1987b), The Dollar as a Speculative Bubble: a Tale of Fundamentalists and Chartists, *Greek Economic Review*, pp. 49 - 102.

Frankel, Jeffrey A. and Kenneth Froot (1990), Chartists, Fundamentalists and Trading in Foreign Exchange Markets, *The American Economic Review, Papers and Proceedings*, pp. 181 - 185.

Frankel, Jeffrey A. and Andrew K. Rose (1995), A Survey of Empirical Research on Nominal Exchange Rates, in: Grossman, S., and K. Rogoff (eds.), The Handbook of International Economics, Amsterdam.

Fratzscher, Marcel (2006), On the Long-Term Effectiveness of Exchange Rate Communication and Interventions, *Journal of International Money and Finance* 25, pp. 146 - 167.

Friedman, Milton (1953), The Case for Flexible Exchange Rates, in Essays on Positive Economics, Chicago: University of Chicago press, pp. 157 - 203.

Froot, Kenneth A. and Takatoshi Ito (1989), On the Consistency of Short-Run and Long-Run Exchange Rate Expectations, *Journal of International Money and Finance* 8, pp. 487 - 510.

Froot, Kenneth A. and Richard H. Thaler (1990), Anomalies: Foreign Exchange, *Journal of Economic Perspectives* 4 (3), pp. 179 - 192.

Gabriele Galati, Alexandra Heath and Patrick McGuire (2007), Evidence of Carry Trade Activity, *BIS Quarterly Review*, September, pp. 27 - 41.

Gallagher, Liam and Mark P. Taylor (2001), Risky Arbitrage, Limits of Arbitrage and Nonlinear Adjustment in the Dividend-Price Ratio, *Economic Inquiry* 39, pp. 524 - 536.

Giordani, Paul and Paul Soederlind (2001), Inflation Forecast Uncertainty, Stockholm School of Economics EFI Working Paper No. 384.

Granger, Clive W. and Timo Teräsvirta (1993), Modeling Nonlinear Economic Relationships, Oxford University Press, Oxford.

Greer, Mark (1999), Assessing the Soothsayers: An Examination of the Track Record of Macroeconomic Forecasting, *Journal of Economic Issues* 28 (1), pp. 77 - 94.

Greer, Mark (2003), Directional Accuracy Tests of Long-Term Interest Rate Forecasts, *International Journal of Forecasting* 19 (2), pp. 291 - 298.

Hamalainen, Nell (2004), A Survey of Taylor-Type Monetary Policy Rules, Canadian Department of Finance, Working Paper 2004-02.

Heppke-Falk, Kerstin, and Felix Huefner (2004), Expected Budget Deficits and Interest Rate Swap Spreads - Evidence for France, Germany and Italy, Deutsche Bundesbank Discussion Paper No 40/2004.

Honohan, Patrick (1984), Expectation Errors and Exchange-Rate Volatility, *Journal of Macroeconomics* 6 (3), pp. 323 - 334.

Hopkins, Sandra and Jonathon Murphy (1997), Do Interventions Contain Information? Evidence from the Australian Foreign Exchange Market, *Australian Journal of Management* 22 (2), pp. 199 - 218.

Hutcheson, Tiffany (2003), Exchange rate movements as explained by dealers, *Economic Papers* 22 (3), pp. 35 - 46.

Ito, Takatoshi (1990), Foreign Exchange Expectations: Micro Survey Data, *The American Economic Review*, pp. 434-449.

Ito, Takatoshi (1993), Foreign Exchange Rate Expectations: Micro Survey Data, in: Das, Dilip K. (ed.), International Finance: Contemporary Issues, Routledge, pp. 360 - 374.

Jeong, Jinook and George S. Maddala (1991), Measurement Errors and Tests for Rationality, *Journal of Business and Economic Statistics* 9 (4), pp. 431 - 439.

Jongen, Ron, Verschoor, Willem F.C. and Christian C. P. Wolff (2008), Foreign Exchange Rate Expectations: Survey and Synthesis, *Journal of economic surveys* 22 (1), pp. 140-165.

Judd, John P., Glenn D. Rudebusch (1998), Taylor Rules and the Fed: 1970-1997, *FRBSF Economic Review* 3, pp. 3 - 16.

Juuttner D. Johannes and Roger Tonkin (1992), Intervention in foreign currency markets: A task for Sisyphus?, Economics Research Paper # 353, Macquarie University.

Kaminski, Graciela L. and Karen K. Lewis (1996), Does Foreign Exchange Intervention Signal Future Monetary Policy?, *Journal of Monetary Economics* 37, pp. 285 - 312.

Karunaratne, Neil D. (1996), Exchange Rate Intervention in Australia (December 1983 to May 1993), *Journal of Policy Modeling* 18 (4), pp. 397 - 417.

Keane, Michael P. and David E. Runkle (1990), Testing the Rationality of Price Forecasts: New Evidence from Panel Data, *The American Economic Review* 80, pp. 714 - 735.

Kearns Jonathan and Roberto Rigobon (2005), Identifying the Efficacy of Central Bank Interventions: Evidence from Australia and Japan, *Journal of International Economics* 66, pp. 31 - 48.

Krueger, James and Kenneth Kuettner (1996), The Fed Funds Rate as a Predictor of Federal Reserve Policy, *Journal of Future Markets* 16, pp. 865 - 879.

Kilian, Lutz and Mark P. Taylor, (2003), Why Is It So Difficult to Beat the Random Walk Forecast of Exchange Rates?, *Journal of International Economics* 60, pp. 85 - 107.

Kim, Suk-Joong, Kortian, Tro and Jeffrey Sheen (2000), Central bank Intervention and Exchange Rates Volatility - Australian Evidence, *Journal of International Financial Markets, Institutions and Money* 10, pp. 381 - 405.

Kim, Suk-Joong and Cyril M. D. Pham (2006), Is Foreign Exchange Intervention by Central Banks Bad News for Debt Markets?: A Case of Reserve Bank of Australia's Intervention 1986 - 2003, *Journal of International Financial Markets, Institutions and Money* 16, pp. 446 - 467.

Kim, Suk-Joong and Jeffrey Sheen (2002), The Determinants of Foreign Exchange Intervention by Central Banks: Evidence from Australia, *Journal of International Money and Finance* 21, pp. 619 - 649.

Kolb, Richard A. and Henry O. Stekler (1996), Is There a Consensus among Financial Forecasters?, *International Journal of Forecasting*, 12 (4), pp. 455 - 564.

Krueger, Joel T. and Ken N. Kuttner (1996), The Fed Funds Future Rates as a Predictor of Federal Reserve Policy, *Journal of Future Markets* 16, pp. 865 - 879.

Landerrechte, Oscar, Corbo, Vittorio and Klaus Schmidt-Hebbel (2001), Does Inflation Targeting make a Difference?, Central Bank of Chile Working Paper No. 106.

Lewis, Karen K. (1999), Trying to Explain Home Bias in Equities and Consumption, *Journal of Economic Literature* 37, pp. 571 - 608.

Laster, David, Bennett, Paul and In Sun Geoum (1999), Rational Bias in Macroeconomic Forecasts, *The Quarterly Journal of Economics* 114 (1), pp. 293 - 318.

Leitner, Johannes, Robert Schmidt and Peter Bofinger (2003), Biases of Professional Exchange Rate Forecasts: Psychological Explanations and an Experimentally Based Comparison to Novices, Würzburg Economic Papers #39.

Levin, Andrew T., Natalucci, Fabio M. and Jeremy M. Piger (2004), The Macroeconomic Effects of Inflation Targeting, Federal Reserve Bank of St. Louis Review 86 (4), pp. 51 - 80.

Liu, Peter C. and George S. Maddala (1992), Rationality of Survey Data and Tests for Market Efficiency in the Foreign Exchange Markets, *Journal of International Money and Finance* 11 (4), pp. 366 - 381.

Lundbergh, Stefan and Timo Teräsvirta (1998), Modeling Economic High Frequency Time Series With STAR GARCH Models, Stockholm School of Economics, Working Paper No. 291.

Lux, Thomas (1998), The Socio-Economic Dynamics of Speculative Markets: Interacting Agents, Chaos and Fat Tails of Return, *Journal of Economic Behavior and Organization* 33, pp. 143 - 165.

Lyons, Richard (1997), A Simultaneous Trade Model of the Foreign Exchange Hot Potato, *Journal of International Economics* 42, pp. 275 - 298.

MacDonald, Ronald (2000), Expectation Formation and Risk in Three Financial Markets: Surveying What The Survey Says, *Journal of Economic Surveys* 14 (1), pp. 69 - 100.

MacDonald, Ronald and Ian W. Marsh (1996), Currency Forecasters Are Heterogeneous: Confirmation and Consequences, *Journal of International Money and Finance* 15, pp. 665 - 685.

MacDonald, Ronald and Thomas S. Torrance, (1988), On Risk, Rationality and Excessive Speculation in the Deutschmark-US Dollar Exchange Market: Some Evidence using Survey Data, *Oxford Bulletin of Economics and Statistics* 50 (2), pp. 107 - 123.

Makin, Arnold J., and Jacob Shaw (1997), The Ineffectiveness of Foreign Exchange Intervention in Australia, *Asian Economies* 26, pp. 82 - 96.

Meese, Richard A. and Kenneth Rogoff (1983), Empirical Exchange Rate Models of the Seventies: Do They Fit out of Sample?, *Journal of International Economics* 14 (1 - 2), pp. 3 - 24.

Menkhoff, Lukas (1998), The Noise Trading Approach - Questionnaire Evidence from Foreign Exchange, *Journal of International Money and Finance* 17, pp. 547 - 564.

Menkhoff, Lukas (2001), Short-Term Horizons in Foreign Exchange? - Survey Evidence from Dealers and Fund Managers, *Kyklos* 54, pp. 27 - 47.

Menkhoff, Lukas, and Mark P. Taylor (2007), The Obstinate Passion of Foreign Exchange Professionals: Technical Analysis, *Journal of Economic Literature*, 45 (4), pp. 936 - 972.

McKenzie, Michael D. (2004), An Empirical Examination of the Relationship between Central Bank Intervention and Exchange Rate Volatility: Some Australian Evidence, *Australian Economic Papers* 43 (1), pp. 59 - 74.

Mishkin, Frederic S. and Klaus Schmidt-Hebbel (2006), Does Inflation Targeting make a difference?, Central Bank of Chile Working Paper No. 404.

Mitchell, Karlyn and Douglas K. Pearce (2007a), Professional Forecasts of Interest Rates and Exchange Rates: Evidence from the Wall Street Journal's Panel of Economists, *Journal of Macroeconomics* 29 (3), pp. 840 - 854.

Mitchell, Karlyn and Douglas K. Pearce (2007b), Do Wall Street Economists Believe in Okun's Law and the Taylor Rule?, Working Paper, North Carolina State University.

Moosa, Imad A. and Abul Shamsuddin (2004), Expectation Formation Mechanisms, Profitability of Foreign Exchange Trading and Exchange Rate Volatility, *Applied Economics* 36 (14), pp. 1599 - 1606.

Mussa, Michael L. (1981), The Role of Official Intervention, Occasional Paper 6, New York: Group of Thirty.

Neely, Christopher J. (2000), The Practice of Central Bank Intervention: Looking Under the Hood, *Central Banking* 11 (2), pp. 24 - 37.

Neely, Christopher J. (2005), An Analysis of Recent Studies of the Effect of Foreign Exchange Intervention, *Federal Reserve Bank of St. Louis Review*, November/December 2005, 87 (6), pp. 685 - 717.

Neely, Chistopher J. (2006), Authorities' Belief about Foreign Exchange Intervention: Getting Back Under the Hood, Federal Reserve Bank of St. Louis, working paper, July 2006.

O'Hara, Maureen (2005), Market Microstructure Theory, Malden, Blackwell.

Orphanides, Anthanasios (2001), Monetary Policy Rules based on Real-Time Data, *The American Economic Review* 91 (4), pp. 964 - 985.

Osterberg, William P. (2000), New Results on the Rationality of Survey Measures of Exchange Rate Expectations, *Federal Reserve Bank of Cleveland Economic Review* 36 (1), pp. 14 - 21.

Ozaki, Takatoshi (1985), Nonlinear Time Series Models and Dynamic Systems, in: Hannan, Edward J., Krishnaiah, Paul R. and Michael M. Rao (eds.), Handbook of Statistics 5, pp. 25 - 83, Amsterdam, Elsevier.

Peiers, Bettina (1997), Informed Traders, Intervention, and Price Leadership: A Deeper View of the Microstructure of the Foreign Exchange Market, *Journal of Finance* 52, pp. 1589 - 1614.

Rankin, Robert (1998), The Exchange Rate and the Reserve Bank's Role in the Foreign Exchange Market, Reserve Bank of Australia, unpublished manuscript.

Reade, J. James (2006), The Taylor Rule in a Real-Time Cointegrated VAR Model of the US, Working Paper, Oxford University.

Reitz, Stefan and Mark P. Taylor (2008a), The Coordination Channel of Foreign Exchange Intervention: A Nonlinear Microstructural Analysis, *European Economic Review*, 52, pp. 55 - 76.

Reitz, Stefan and Mark P. Taylor (2008b), Nonlinear Impact of Central Bank Intervention: Empirical Evidence from Yen/US-Dollar Exchange Rates, *International Journal of Finance and Economics*, forthcoming.

Reitz, Stefan and Frank Westerhoff (2003), Nonlinearities and cyclical behavior. The role of chartists and fundamentalists, *Studies in Nonlinear Dynamics & Econometrics* 7, pp. 1125 - 1172.

Reserve Bank of Australia (1984, 2000, 2003, 2004), various annual reports.

Romer, Christina D. and David H. Romer (2002), A Rehabilitation of Monetary Policy in the 1950s, *The American Economic Review* 92, pp. 121 - 127.

Roger, Jeff M. and Pierre L. Siklos (2003), Foreign Exchange Market Intervention in Two Small Open Economies: The Canadian and Australian Experience, *Journal of International Money and Finance* 22, pp. 393 - 416.

Rosenberg, Michael R. (2003), Exchange Rate Determination: Models and Strategies for Exchange Rate Forecasting, New York: McGraw-Hill.

Rudebusch, Glenn D. (2006), Monetary Policy Inertia - Fact or Fiction?, *International Journal of Central Banking* 2, pp. 85 - 135.

Sager, Michael and Mark P. Taylor (2006), Under the Microscope: The Structure of the Foreign Exchange Market, *International Journal of Finance and Economics*, 11 (1), pp. 81 - 95.

Sarno, Lucio and Mark P. Taylor (2001), Official Intervention in the Foreign Exchange Market: Is It Effective and, If So, How Does It Work?, *Journal of Economic Literature*, 39 (3), pp. 839 - 868.

Schmidt-Hebbel, Klaus and Alejandro Werner (2002), Inflation Targeting in Brazil, Chile, and Mexico: Performance, Credibility, and the Exchange Rate, *Economia* 2 (2), pp. 31 - 89.

Schwartz, Anna J. (2000), The Rise and Fall of Foreign Exchange Market Intervention as a policy tool, *Journal of Financial Services Research* 18, pp. 319 - 339.

Shleifer, Andrei and Robert W. Vishny (1997), The Limits of Arbitrage, *Journal of Finance* 52 (1), pp. 35 - 55.

Söderlind, Paul (2000), Market Expectations in the UK Before and After the ERM Crisis, *Economica* 67, pp. 1 - 18.

Stadtmann, Georg, Frenkel, Michael and Jan-Christoph Rülke (2006), Erwartungsbildung im Dollar/Euro Devisenmarkt, *Aussenwirtschaft* 61 (3), pp. 277 - 298.

Stekler, Henry O. (2002), The Rationality and Efficiency of Individuals Forecasts, in Clements, Michael P., and David F. Hendry (eds.), A Companion to Economic Forecasting, pp. 222 - 240, Oxford, Blackwell.

Svensson, Lars E.O. (1997), Inflation Forecast Targeting: Implementing and Monitoring Inflation Targets, *European Economic Review* 41, pp. 1111-1146.

Takagi, Shinji (1991), Exchange Rate Expectations, a Survey of Survey Studies, *IMF staff papers* 38, pp. 156 - 183.

Taylor, John B. (1993), Discretion versus Policy Rules in Practice, Carnegie-Rochester Conference Series on Public Policy 39, pp. 195 - 214.

Taylor, John B. (1999), A Historical Analysis of Monetary Policy Rules, in: Taylor, John B. (ed.), Monetary Policy Rules, University of Chicago Press.

Taylor, Mark P. (1987), Covered Interest Parity: A High Frequency, High Quality Data Study, *Economica* 54, pp. 429 - 438.

Taylor, Mark P. (1989), Covered Interest Arbitrage and Market Turbulence, *Economic Journal* 99, pp. 376 - 391.

Taylor, Mark P. (1995), The Economics of Exchange Rates, *Journal of Economic Literature* 33, pp. 13 - 47.

Taylor, Mark P. (2004), Is Official Exchange Rate Intervention Effective?, *Economica* 71, pp. 1 - 11.

Taylor, Mark P. (2005), Official Foreign Exchange Intervention as a Coordinating Signal in the Dollar-Yen Market, *Pacific Economic Review* 10 (1), pp. 73 - 82.

Taylor, Mark P. and Helen Allen (1992), The Use of Technical Analysis in the Foreign Exchange Market, *Journal of International Money and Finance* 11 (3), pp. 304 - 314.

Taylor, Mark P. and David A. Peel (2000), Nonlinear Adjustment, Long-Run Equilibrium and Exchange Rate Fundamentals, *Journal of International Money and Finance* 19, pp. 33 - 53.

Taylor, Mark P., Peel, David A. and Lucio Sarno (2001), Nonlinear Mean Reversion in Real Exchange Rates: Toward a Solution to the Purchasing Power Parity Puzzles, *International Economic Review* 42, pp. 1015 - 1042.

Teräsvirta, Timo and Heather M. Anderson (1992), Characterizing Nonlinearities in Business Cycles using Smooth Transition Autoregressive Models, *Journal of Applied Econometrics* 7, pp. 119 - 139.

Teräsvirta, Timo (1994), Specification, Estimation, and Evaluation of Smooth Transition Autoregressive Models, *Journal of American Statistical Association* 89, pp. 208 - 218.

Trippi, Robert R. and Richard B. Harriff (1993), Trading Volume, Heterogeneity of Expectations, and the Disperson of Volatilities implied by Option Prices, *Review of Quantitative Finance and Accounting* 3 (3), pp. 339 - 351.

Westermann, Frank and Michael M. Hutchinson (2006), Japan's Great Stagnation, Financial and Monetary Policy Lessons for Advanced Economies, MIT Press.

Wooldridge, Jeffrey M. (2002), Econometric Analysis of Cross Section and Panel Data, Cambridge, MIT Press.

Appendix A: Derivation of consistency restrictions for a distributed lag function with one lag

Starting from

(A1) $$E_t[s_{t+1}] - s_t = \alpha_1 + \beta_1(s_{t-1} - s_t) + \epsilon_t$$

and

(A2) $$E_t[s_{t+2}] - s_t = \alpha_2 + \beta_2(s_{t-1} - s_t) + u_t$$

and after rearranging, this yields into

(A3) $$E_t[s_{t+1}] = \alpha_1 + (1 - \beta_1)s_t + \beta_1 s_{t-1} + \epsilon_t.$$

(A4) $$E_t[s_{t+2}] = \alpha_2 + (1 - \beta_2)s_t + \beta_2 s_{t-1} + u_t.$$

By iterating the short-term expectation, the expectation of a longer time horizon can be obtained. With the information available at time t, the following substitution can be derived:

(A5) $$E_{t+1}[s_{t+2}] = \alpha_1 + (1 - \beta_1)E_t[s_{t+1}] + \beta_1 s_t,$$

where

(A6) $$E_t[s_{t+1}] = \alpha_1 + (1 - \beta_1)s_t + \beta_1 s_{t-1} + \epsilon_t.$$

Finally, from $(A1)$ to $(A5)$, we obtain

(A7) $$E_{t+1}[s_{t+2}] = \alpha_1 + (1 - \beta_1)[\alpha_1 + (1 - \beta_1)s_t + \beta_1 s_{t-1}] + \beta_1 s_t.$$

Rearranging yields

(A8) $$E_{t+1}[s_{t+2}] = 2\alpha_1 - \alpha_1\beta_1 + s_t(1 - \beta_1 + {\beta_1}^2) + s_{t-1}(\beta_1 - {\beta_1}^2).$$

Hence, consistent long-term forecasts must comply with the following restrictions:

(R1) $$\alpha_2 = 2\alpha_1 - \alpha_1\beta_1$$

(R2) $$\beta_2 = \beta_1(1 - \beta_1)$$

Appendix B: Derivation of consistency restrictions for a distributed lag function with two lags

Considering the following short-term and long-term expectation formations, the consistency restrictions can be derived by starting from the equations:

(B1) $$E_t[s_{t+1}] - s_t = \alpha_1 + \beta_1 s_t + \gamma_1 s_{t-1} + \delta_1 s_{t-2} + \phi_t$$

(B2) $$E_t[s_{t+2}] - s_t = \alpha_2 + \beta_2 s_t + \gamma_2 s_{t-1} + \delta_2 s_{t-2} + \chi_t$$

Rearranging yields

(B3) $$E_t[s_{t+1}] = \alpha_1 + (1 + \beta_1) s_t + \gamma_1 s_{t-1} + \delta_1 s_{t-2} + \phi_t$$

(B4) $$E_t[s_{t+2}] = \alpha_2 + (1 + \beta_2) s_t + \gamma_2 s_{t-1} + \delta_2 s_{t-2} + \chi_t$$

where ϕ_t and χ_t are error terms. We can now derive consistency restrictions for extrapolative expectations with two lags. From $(B.3)$, we know that

(B5) $$E_{t+1}[s_{t+2}] = \alpha_1 + (1 + \beta_1) E_t[s_{t+1}] + \gamma_1 s_t + \delta_1 s_{t-1}$$

where

(B6) $$E_t[s_{t+1}] = \alpha_1 + (1 + \beta_1) s_t + \gamma_1 s_{t-1} + \delta_1 s_{t-2}.$$

Finally from $(B.2)$ to $(B.5)$, we obtain

(B7) $$E_{t+1}[s_{t+2}] = \alpha_1 + (1+\beta_1)[\alpha_1 + (1+\beta_1) s_t + \gamma_1 s_{t-1} + \delta_1 s_{t-2}] + \gamma s_t + \delta_1 s_{t-1}.$$

Rearranging yields

(B8) $$E_{t+1}[s_{t+2}] - s_t = 2\alpha_1 + \alpha_1\beta_1 + s_t(2\beta_1 + {\beta_1}^2 + \gamma_1) + s_{t-1}(\beta_1\gamma_1 + \gamma_1 + \delta_1) + s_{t-2}(\delta_1 + \beta_1\delta_1).$$

Hence, consistent long-term forecasts must comply with the following restrictions:

(R3) $$\alpha_2 = 2\alpha_1 + \alpha_1\beta_1$$

(R4) $$\beta_2 = 2\beta_1 + {\beta_1}^2 + \gamma_1$$

(R5) $$\gamma_2 = \beta_1\gamma_1 + \gamma_1 + \delta_1$$

(R6) $$\delta_2 = \delta_1 + \beta_1\delta_1$$

Appendix C: Calculation of the weighted average of expected GDP and CPI

In order to generate a three months forecast we set the forecasted variable f_t at time t (= 1,2,.., 219) equal to the forecast of the current year f_t^{cur} if the forecast is provided before November (i.e. the remaining three months are all part of the current year). If the forecast is provided in November or December the three month forecast f_t is calculated as a weighted arithmetic average of the forecast for the current year f_t^{cur} and the next year f_t^{next}. We weight the forecast f_t with the remaining number of months m (with $m = 2$ (for November forecasts) and $m = 1$ (for December forecasts)) at the time of the forecast t:

(C1) $$f_t = \frac{f_t^{cur} * m + (3-m) * f_t^{next}}{3}$$

In order to generate a twelve months forecast horizon which is consistent with the forecast horizon of the twelve months interest rate forecast we apply the outlined procedure with 1 (= December) $\leq$ m $\leq$ 12 (= January). The twelve months GDP and CPI forecasts f_t are as follows:

(C2) $$f_t = \frac{f_t^{cur} * m + (12-m) * f_t^{next}}{12}$$

This procedure has been applied by Heppke-Falk and Hüffner (2004) too and Beck (2001). Both studies also use data of the Economics Consensus Inc. and construct the arithmetic average as outlined above

Studien zu Internationalen Wirtschaftsbeziehungen

Herausgegeben von Prof. Dr. Michael Frenkel

Band 1 Christiane Nickel: Insider und Outsider bei der Osterweiterung der Europäischen Währungsunion. 2002.

Band 2 Georg Stadtmann: Noise-Trader auf Devisenmärkten. Viel Lärm um Nichts? 2002.

Band 3 Wolf-Heimo Grieben: Trade and Technology as Competing Explanations for Rising Inequality. An Endogenous Growth Perspective. 2003.

Band 4 Alexander Mende: Order Flow Analyses and Foreign Exchange Dealing. 2005.

Band 5 Torsten Wezel: Determinants of Foreign Direct Investment in Emerging Markets. An Empirical Study of FDI Flows from Germany and its Banking Sector. 2005.

Band 6 Steffen Kern: The Behaviour of Interest Groups in Trade and Industry Towards Monetary Policy and Central Banks. Theory and Evidence on Germany and the Euro Area. 2006.

Band 7 Holger Michaelis: Kapitalbilanzliberalisierung in der Volksrepublik China und ihre Einbettung in den volkswirtschaftlichen Reformprozess. 2006.

Band 8 Ralf Fendel: Monetary Policy, Interest Rate Rules, and the Term Structure of Interest Rates. Theoretical Considerations and Empirical Implications. 2007.

Band 9 Katja Funke: Balance of Payments Issues in Central and Eastern European Countries' Run-Up to Euro Area Accession. 2007.

Band 10 Isabell Koske: Equilibrium Exchange Rate Models, the Euro and the 2004 Expansion of the EU. 2007.

Band 11 Dennis Stremmel: Protektionsmöglichkeiten in der WTO? Geistige Eigentumsrechte im TRIPs-Abkommen und die Forderung nach Sozial- und Umweltstandards. 2007.

Band 12 Daniela Beckmann: From Early Warning Systems to Asset Managers' Behavior: Evidence for Mature and Emerging Markets. 2008.

Band 13 Markus A. Schmidt: Information or Market Power: What is Governing Dealers' Pricing Behaviour in FX Markets? An Investigation in the Spirit of the Microstructure Approach to Exchange Rates. 2008.

Band 14 Jan-Christoph Rülke: Expectations in Financial Markets – A Survey Data Approach. 2009.

www.peterlang.de

FSC
www.fsc.org
MIX
Papier | Fördert gute Waldnutzung
FSC® C083411

Kolibri 360 GmbH
Ferdinand-Jühlke-Straße 7
99095 Erfurt, Deutschland
produktsicherheit@kolibri360.de